THE OBSERVER'S BOOK OF

WILD FLOWERS

Compiled by

W. J. STOKOE

Describing
TWO HUNDRED BRITISH SPECIES
with 220 illustrations
100 of which are in full colour

D1197805

FREDERICK WARNE & CO. LTD.
FREDERICK WARNE & CO. INC.
LONDON · NEW YORK

7232 0044 0

Printed in Great Britain

PREFACE

This little book is intended for the pocket to enable the observer in his wanderings through field and woodland, to study the wonderful variety of wild flowers around him. It is not intended to take the place of the more complete works on the subject, but it is hoped that it will awaken and intensify the interest sufficiently for all those seekers after the beauties of nature to take up this absorbing subject for a more serious and deeper study.

In a work of this extent, it will be obvious that it must necessitate an economical selection of species, and this has been most carefully carried out, with an eye to those plants which are easily accessible and more or less abundant and most likely to be found during a walk in the open country.

The essential botanical descriptions given, will be found sufficient to enable the name and species to be easily recognized, and will greatly assist the flower-lover, with the aid of a good pocket-lens, to lay bare the secrets of the flowers, so cunningly devised by nature, for their preservation and propagation.

The compiler desires to express to Messrs. Frederick Warne & Co., Ltd., his thanks for their kind permission to use, and make extracts from, the popular standard work *Wayside and Woodland Blossoms*, by Edward Step, F.L.S., and also for the use of the beautiful illustrations, reproduced, in small size, from *Sowerby's English Botany*, which have been specially prepared for this work.

W. J. STOKOE.

INTRODUCTION

In the descriptions of the species selected in this work, the shapes of the leaves and the parts of a flower are indicated, as far as possible, in ordinary language. A series of diagrams representing the principal forms of leaves is given in the Glossary, together with a short explanation, to facilitate easy reference.

In giving a description of the parts of a flower and a brief account of the principal kinds of flower grouping, it may be pointed out that this grouping is directly influenced by the connection between plant and insect. For instance, the smaller blossoms co-operate among themselves with the object of rendering them conspicuous, though individually they are very often insignificant. By the simple expedient of mounting these small flowers upon radiating footstalks of varying lengths, a hundred or more flowers are brought together on a common level, and thus they form, not only to the human rambler but to the insect world also, some of the most conspicuous flower-masses of our hedgerows.

It will be found that many flowers lay themselves out specially to attract the night-flying moths, and with this object in view, they are most frequently pure white and therefore very conspicuous.

But not only are plants specially adapted to encourage the visits of particular groups of insects, but many of them take pains to exclude unprofitable visitors of the smaller kind, who would simply steal nectar or pollen without rendering any service in return. And so, for instance, when Nature makes the tubular bell of the Foxglove just sufficiently large to enable a big humble-bee to enter and well dust itself with pollen, she also takes care to plant a barrier of long hairs in the entrance, which small and unwanted insects cannot pass. Then, again, the periods of the opening and closing of many flowers have relation to the time of day at which the pollen-carrying insect flies, and even the very manner in which a flower is hung might, in most cases, be similarly explained.

It is to be hoped that these few specific instances will serve to whet the appetite of the flower-lover, and create a desire for a deeper knowledge of this most interesting subject, by more closely considering the growing plant, before plucking the flower.

Regarding the forms of flowers, a diagram of a section of an imaginary flower, with its parts clearly marked, followed by definitions, is here given.

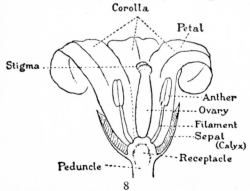

Commencing from the flower-stalk (*peduncle*), whose large, fleshy head is known as the *receptacle*, there is the first series of floral organs, the *sepals*, known collectively as the *calyx*, and the succeeding series, the *petals*, forming the *corolla*.

Sometimes all the *sepals* and all the *petals* are joined together to form a tube or a cup, but usually in those cases their number is indicated by the lobes on the free margin. Within the *corolla* there is a series of very dissimilar organs, as shown by the following diagram.

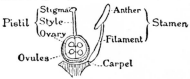

The *stamens* and within these the *pistil*. The *stamen* consists of two portions, the *filament* or stalk, and the *anther* or pollen sac. *Pollen* is the mealy powder—the male element—by contact with which the *ovules* are fertilized. These ovules are contained in the lower portion of the central or female organ. This—the *pistil*—consists of three portions, the enlarged base or *ovary* composed of one or more *carpels*, and containing one or more ovules. The slender *style* which is often absent ; and its more or less viscid or hairy summit, the *stigma*. The stigma may be divided into two, three or more lobes, which correspond with the number of carpels of which the ovary is composed.

Thus, briefly, is described the ordinary structure of flowers. An illustrated Glossary of botanical terms, with full definitions, is now given.

GLOSSARY

Achene.—A fruit like a little nut.

Annual.—Plants flowering in the same year as they are raised from seed.

Arrow-shaped leaf.—A wide base, with two pointed lobes directed downwards.

Arrow-shaped.

Awl-shaped leaf.—Tapering from a thicker base to a fine point.

Axil.—The angle between the stem and leaf-stalk.

Biennial.—Flowering only in the year following that in which they are sown.

Bract.—A modified leaf beneath a flower.

Bracteole.—A diminutive bract.

Carpel.—A division of the ovary or seed-vessel.

Clasping leaf.—When a stalkless leaf encircles the stem.

Bract.

Compound.—A leaf broken up into several leaflets.

Connate.—When the bases of opposite leaves are grown together.

Corymb.—Where the cluster of flowers is brought more or less to the same level.

Connate Leaves.

Cyme.—A shoot terminating in a flower, then sending off side branches, each of which terminate in like manner.

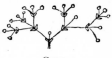

Cyme.

Digitate leaf.—Leaflets radiating from the leaf-stalk.

Dimorphic.—Flowers that appear in two forms.

Diœcious.—When staminate and pistillate flowers are borne by different plants of a species.

Elliptical leaf.—Oval shape and tapering both ends.

Entire leaf.—Having the margin undivided.

Entire Leaf.

Filament.—The stalk-like portion of the stamen.

Follicle.—A dry one-celled and one-valved fruit, containing more than one seed.

Genera.—The plural of *genus*.

Genus.—An assemblage of species, which all agree in *one or more* important structural characters.

Heart-shaped leaf.—Broad, with two rounded lobes.

Heart-shaped.

Inferior.—Denotes that the calyx or corolla is free from and below the ovary.

Inflorescence.—The grouping of flowers on a plant.

Involucre.—A series of bract-like leaves below a cluster of flowers.

Involucre.

12

Kidney-shaped leaf. — Heart-shape with the tip rounded.

Lance-shaped leaf.—The lower end broad gradually tapering to the tip.

Leaflets. — When there are several succeeding each other on each side of the midrib.

Leaflets.

Linear leaf.—Long and very narrow, with parallel sides.

Node.—A point of the stem whence leaves arise.

Oblong leaf.—Twice as long as broad, with both ends rounded.

Order.—A group of *genera*, all of which agree in some striking particular.

Oblong Leaf.

Oval or Egg-shaped leaf.—Tapering to each end.

Palmate leaf.—Lobed in the form of a hand.

Panicle.—When the pedicels are branched, supporting two or more flowers in a loose cluster.

Oval Leaves.

Pedicel.—A flower-stalk supporting several flowers without footstalks.

Perennial. — Rootstocks that increase and expand yearly.

Perianth. — Flowers showing no distinction between calyx and corolla.

Panicle.

Perfoliate leaf.—When a stem passes through the base of a stalkless leaf.

Pinnate leaf.—Leaflets of elongate shape, forming pairs on opposite sides.

Pinnatified leaf.—When the leaf is deeply cut into lobes.

Perfoliate leaves.

Raceme.—Flowers arranged like a spike, but with footstalks.

Radical leaves.—Leaves that rise directly from the rootstock.

Scape. — A flower-stalk arising directly from the rootstock.

Sessile.—Leaves or flowers connected with the stem without footstalks.

Raceme.

Simple leaf.—An undivided leaf.

Spadix.—An inflorescence where the flowers are arranged round a thick, fleshy spike.

Spathe.—The large bract that envelops certain flowers before opening.

Simple Leaf.

Species.—Individual plants bearing certain characters in common.

Spike.—Bearing a number of flowers without footstalks.

Spoon-shaped leaf.—The broadest part at the tip and tapering to the base.

Spike.

Spreading.—When the petals of a flower are at right angles with the central column. Hairs standing out horizontally.

Stipules.—Small leaves, always in pairs, at the base of the leaf-stalk.

Sword-shaped leaf.—An erect leaf which has thickness as well as length and narrowness.

Terminal.—Flowers produced at the summit of a stem or end of a branch.

Trefoil.—A simple form of division.

Tubercle.—A small swelling; a little knob.

Umbel.—A flat-topped cluster of flowers, having their foot-stalks of pretty equal length and radiating like the ribs of an umbrella.

Versatile.—When the anther is so connected to the filament, that it swings freely, as if balanced on a pivot.

Stipules.

Trefoil.

Umbels.

MEADOW-RUE

Family RANUNCULACEAE   *Thalictrum flavum*

The largest and most striking of our native species. It is found in swampy fields and on the banks of rivers and streams.

Its distribution extends from the South of England to Scotland; it occurs only locally in Ireland.

The annual stems are stout and furrowed and rise to a height of from two to four feet from a perennial creeping rootstock which sends out runners. The smooth leaves are broken into three stalked divisions and each of these into paired leaflets which are wedge-shaped and end in three lobes.

All the bright yellow flowers are upright on their stalks, their brightness really due to the twenty-four spreading stamens. The four small sepals are cream-coloured and the carpels are of the achene type, from six to ten of them, each producing a single seed.

There is no provision of nectar, but the flowers are visited by insects for the sake of their abundant pollen.

Flowering in July and August.

TRAVELLER'S JOY

Family RANUNCULACEAE   *Clematis vitalba*

In chalky districts especially, this climbing shrub will be met with at every turn, scrambling over the hedges, clinging persistently to every branch or shoot it touches. In autumn, when the feathery awns are lengthening on its seed-vessels, it is aptly called "Old Man's Beard."

It is a perennial plant, and is found only to the south of Denbigh and Stafford. The stem is tough, and it climbs by means of its leafstalks which curl round any likely support and become hard as wire.

The leaves are opposite and compound, the leaflets usually five. The slightly fragrant flowers have no corolla, but the four thick, downy sepals are coloured greenish-white to serve instead. The stamens are a crowd round the central cluster of many-bearded styles, which afterwards elongate into plumy tails and jointly form the "Old Man's Beard."

It is the only British member of the genus; but a large number of foreign species, with larger flowers, are cultivated in our gardens.

Flowering from July to September.

WOOD ANEMONE

Family RANUNCULACEAE　　　*Anemone nemorosa*

One of the earliest of spring flowers to be found in copses, by the woodside and in upland meadows.

It is perennial, and the creeping rootstock sends up its stems with folded leaves and drooping buds.

Half-way up the stem there are three wedge-shaped involucral leaves. The ordinary leaves are similar, but they are produced at a little distance from the flower-stalks and do not rise until the flowers have expanded.

The flower has one series of floral leaves, coloured like petals but regarded as sepals. They are white, tinged with pink inside and marked with purple outside—so hung that they turn their backs to the slightest breeze. The sepals may number from four to nine, normally five, frequently six. In the centre is a head of pistils, each with its short, straight style, and these are surrounded with a ring of stamens. The fruits consist of little nut-like achenes, which contain a single seed.

Flowering from March to June.

PHEASANT'S EYE

Family RANUNCULACEAE   *Adonis annua*

Beyond being well-established in Suffolk and the Southern Counties, it is not one of our native plants, but an immigrant from the Continent. It is found about the lightened soil of our cornfields, especially those upon a chalky subsoil.

It is an annual. The stem is erect, branching and leafy, attaining a height of eight or ten inches. The stalkless leaves are much divided and subdivided, the ultimate segments being very slender.

The flowers are somewhat globular in form owing to the concavity of the petals. The five spreading sepals are purplish-green and the more erect petals, five to ten, are blood-red with a purplish-black base. Both stamens and carpels are numerous, the latter forming an oval head which lengthens after pollination.

The petals are without the nectar-gland found on their near allies, the Buttercups.

The flowers, which appear as early as May, can be found as late as September.

WATER CROWFOOT

Family RANUNCULACEAE   *Ranunculus aquatilis*

As much divergence of opinion exists as to the classification of many of the aquatic species of *Ranunculus* it would be as well for the beginner to regard the Water Crowfoots met with in pond and stream as *R. aquatilis* until such time as he is able to make a fairly extensive collection upon which he may found his own conclusions.

The form figured here is the species known as *Ranunculus peltatus.*

The floating leaves are kidney-shaped, divided into three lobes and three leaflets ; the submerged leaves finely divided into stiff, hair-like segments with scarcely any footstalk.

The flowers are white, with straight, upright stalks. The petals, five or more, are oval, with a yellow patch at the base ; stamens few.

It occurs in still waters, and ponds are often completely covered with the glossy, floating leaves.

The Water Crowfoot is not acrid, and cattle which have access to shallow waters where this plant grows, will wade out to feed upon it.

Flowering in May and June.

BUTTERCUP

Family RANUNCULACEAE   *Ranunculus bulbosus*

These flowers must be well known to all, and are to be found in meadows, pastures and waste places everywhere.

Known also as the Bulbous Crowfoot, it has a turnip-shaped swelling at the base of the erect stem, which rises from six inches to a foot high. There are no runners.

The leaves are divided into three stalked segments, each one lobed and toothed, the central one extending beyond the others which gives the whole leaf a somewhat ovate form.

The flower-stalk is furrowed, and the burnished, golden-yellow flower consists of distinct sepals and petals, normally five of each. The sepals are turned downwards, nearly or quite touching the stalk. The cup-shaped petal is provided with a little scale towards the base, which forms a pocket containing nectar.

Most of the species possess acrid and poisonous juices which cause them to be avoided by browsing animals.

Flowering from April to July.

22

LESSER CELANDINE

Family RANUNCULACEAE   *Ranunculus ficaria*

The burnished gold stars of this charming little plant will be found as early as February on sunny banks and below pasture hedges or by the roadside.

Its roots produce a large number of cylindrical tubers, each of which is capable of producing a new plant, and reproduction is thus speedily effected.

The leaves vary much in shape and size. The larger springing direct from the rootstock are more or less heart-shaped, marked with whitish patches and sometimes with black or purple-brown blotches. The smaller leaves from the stem may approach the form of an ivy leaf.

The bright golden flower consists of the sepals varying from three to five, usually three, and the petals numbering from seven to twelve. The stamens are numerous as also are the rather large carpels. As in the Buttercups these are in the form of achenes, each containing a single seed.

The species is well distributed throughout the country and may be found in flower until May.

GLOBE FLOWER

Family RANUNCULACEAE   *Trollius europaeus*

The Globe Flower may be found in moist woods and up in the mountains of western and northern counties.

From a perennial root-stock rise the principal leaves on long stalks. The leaves are circular in general outline and cut up into five wedge-shaped segments, which are lobed with toothed edges. The stem leaves are smaller and without stalks.

The flowering-stems vary in height from one foot to two and a half feet high terminating in the solitary globular yellow flower. Each flower is provided with from ten to fifteen sepals which are concave, their tips overlapping. There are a similar number of small strap-shaped petals. Within their circle are numerous stamens surrounding the five or more carpels. Each petal has a glandular pit in which nectar is produced, similar to the Buttercup.

Owing to the closeness of the sepals, only small flies appear to be able to effect an entrance. After fertilization the carpels develop into wrinkled follicles containing numerous angular black seeds.

Flowering from May to August.

STINKING HELLEBORE

Family RANUNCULACEAE   *Helleborus foetidus*

Ramblers in the chalk districts of Southern and Eastern England may come across this curious, rather uncommon, plant.

It is a coarse-growing perennial, its large radical leaves divided into five or six narrow leaflets, those that occur on the upper part of the flowering stem are more or less reduced to the condition of divided bracts.

The flowers are rather puzzling at first sight, for the large purple-bordered sepals quite hide the small tubular petals, which are shorter than the many stamens. The petals are indeed turned into drinking cups, for they are filled with nectar for the delectation of insect visitors.

The flowers are globular until after fertilization, when the stamens and petals drop off and the sepals spread. The flowers are numerous, borne in a loose panicle, and their odour is fetid.

The plant is highly poisonous.

Flowering from February to April.

MARSH MARIGOLD

Family RANUNCULACEAE *Caltha palustris*

In marshes, river-meadows and wet copses in spring, the Marsh Marigold is a very conspicuous plant, and its acquisition by the rambler often results in wet feet. In some districts it is known as the King-cup, and in Scotland it is called the Luckan Gowan.

It has a thick, creeping rootstock and broadly heart-shaped glossy leaves with very large stipules with toothed edges. The leaves increase enormously in size after flowering.

The flower has no petals. There are five enlarged sepals richly golden-coloured and highly burnished. The centre of the cup is occupied by a number of carpels which are surrounded by a crowd of stamens and develop after fertilization into as many follicles containing great store of seeds.

The plant is poisonous, but the unopened flower-buds are sometimes pickled and used as a substitute for capers.

The flowering period usually extends from March to May, but in some places flowers may be found as late as August.

26

COLUMBINE

Family RANUNCULACEAE   *Aquilegia vulgaris*

Although the Columbine is a true native of our woods one should be chary of assuming its wildness when found near existing houses or former dwellings.

It is a perennial and forms a rootstock from which rise the radical leaves in bundles, and from the centre of which rises the flowering-stem.

The long-stalked leaves are divided into two or three parts, each stalked and again cut into small lobed and toothed leaflets.

The long flower-stalks bear many drooping flowers. The flower parts are in fives. The sepals are thin and broad, coloured dull-purple or blue like the petals. The petals terminate at the back in a hollow tube with a knob at the end in which nectar is secreted.

The ovary consists of five carpels, each with its own style and stigma. After fertilization the flower-stalk erects itself and the carpels develop into leathery follicles which split and disclose a large number of greenish-black seeds.

Flowering from May to July.

BARBERRY

Family BERBERIDACEAE   *Berberis vulgaris*

A spiny shrub, growing in hedge and copse, brightening the spot with its strings of yellow flowers, and later in the year with its oblong red berries.

Its shoots attain a height of from six to ten feet. The leaves are egg-shaped, narrowest near the short stalk, with spine-like teeth. The yellow flowers include eight or nine sepals and six petals. The petals are in two series, and at the base of each are two nectar glands.

There are six stamens, the bases of which are highly irritable. Any insect alighting on the stigma can reach the nectar, but it is not easy to do so without touching the base of one of the stamens, which then springs forward and the anthers strike the insect, dusting it with pollen. The insects that set this mechanism in motion are flies, bees and beetles with occasionally a butterfly.

The resulting red berries are about half an inch long, of an acid quality, although an excellent preserve is made from them.

Flowering from April to June.

YELLOW WATER-LILY

Family NYMPHAEACEAE   *Nuphar lutea*

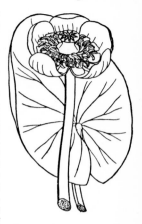

The Yellow Water-lily will be found floating on ponds and sluggish streams. Known, also, as the Brandy-bottle, on account of its flagon-like seed-vessel.

It has a thick, fleshy rootstock, which creeps in the mud and is rich in tannic acid. Some of the leaves are submerged and these are thin, but the floating ones are thick and leathery; heart-shaped and the lobes not far apart. The stalks, somewhat triangular in section, are traversed by a great number of fine air-canals, as are the flower-stalks also, to give them buoyancy.

The flower consists of five or six large yellow sepals which are concave. Petals much smaller, numbering about twenty. They produce nectar at their base. The stamens are even more numerous than the petals, their blunt tips bent over away from the many-celled ovary. The stigma is rayed.

The fruit ripens above water and is flagon-shaped ; the seeds being imbedded in pulp.

The flowering period extends from June to August.

COMMON RED POPPY

Family PAPAVERACEAE   *Papaver rhoeas*

The Common Red Poppy, an annual, one to two feet high, which is so abundant in the cornfields of England and Ireland, less so in Scotland, has branched, bristly stems and pinnate leaves, the points of the lobes directed upward and ending each in a bristle. The bristles on the flower-stalks stand out at right-angles or nearly so. This is an important character.

The flowers are borne on very long and slender stalks, and consist of two concave sepals which are thrown off by the expanding of the two unequal pairs of crumpled petals. The glorious scarlet flowers are from three to four inches in diameter. The pistil, which afterwards develops into the familiar "poppy-head," is surmounted by the many stigmas which form an eight- to twelve-rayed disk. The seed capsule is smooth and short, slightly stalked above the receptacle.

The plants contain a milky juice of a narcotic nature. The flowering period extends from June to September.

WELSH POPPY

Family PAPAVERACEAE   *Meconopsis cambrica*

Although the name suggests that this plant is restricted to Wales, this is not actually the case. Western Poppy would, perhaps, be the more appropriate name for it. Its natural range extends from Yorkshire, southwards through Wales and Somerset to Devon and Cornwall. Its favourite haunts are beside rivulets, moist and shady rocky places.

The Welsh Poppy is perennial with a stout, branching rootstock from which rise, on long stalks, radical leaves, cut into a number of lance-shaped segments which, in turn, are lobed and toothed.

From the stem, which has a woolly base, rise the pale yellow flowers, each on a long footstalk ; the expanded flower measures two or three inches across. There are two hairy sepals and four roundish petals on which lie the numerous stamens encircling the ovary with its four or six rays.

The ovary develops into a seed-capsule with four to six short valves opening below the stigmas for the release of the small wrinkled seeds.

Flowering from June to August.

HORNED POPPY

Family PAPAVERACEAE   *Glaucium flavum*

The Horned Poppy is a near relation of the true Poppies. It is an annual (sometimes perennial) found on sandy seashores where it forms one of the most striking items of vegetation ; frequent on the coasts of England and Ireland, but in Scotland not north of the Firth and Clyde.

It has spreading, branching stems and thick blue-green roughish leaves, large and boldly lobed and cut, clasping the smooth stem by their bases.

The plant attains a height of two feet and the bright yellow flowers are three or four inches across. The two concave sepals that protect the crumpled bud are thrown off when the flower opens and the four petals form two pairs, one pair larger than the other. The ovary is long and narrow, the two-lobed stigma stalkless. The ovary develops into a long two-valved pod, from six inches to one foot in length.

Though only an annual it contrives to flower for about five months, June to October.

GREATER CELANDINE

Family PAPAVERACEAE   *Chelidonium majus*

The Greater Celandine may be found in the hedgerow and on waste ground near habitations. It is not even distantly related to the Lesser Celandine. The former is really a kind of Poppy while the latter is included with the Buttercups.

It is a perennial. The erect branching stems have a yellow juice which is very acrid and poisonous. The handsome leaf is much divided, the leaflets deeply lobed, somewhat resembling an oak leaf.

The rather small yellow flowers, three to six, are combined in umbels and borne on long stalks. There are two sepals and four petals, but the fruit, instead of being an urn-like capsule as in the Poppy, is a long pod with two valves, which separate from the base upwards.

It is regarded by some botanists as an escape from cultivated ground, but it does not appear to be cultivated at the present day.

Flowering from May to August.

WATER-CRESS

Family CRUCIFERAE *Rorippa nasturtium-aquaticum*

A perennial aquatic herb, and one of the best-known of our native plants.

It is found in all districts of the British Isles where there are watercourses or even the mere outflow of a spring.

The hollow stem, under favourable conditions, may be nearly an inch thick and from two to four feet long, floating on the water or creeping on the mud and rooting from the lower side.

The long, narrow leaves consist of three to six pairs of heart-shaped leaflets with a much larger odd leaflet at the end of the midrib.

The small white flowers are clustered in condensed sprays at the ends of the stem or branch. There are four sepals half the length of the four petals, six stamens and a pistil of two united carpels with two short styles. As fertilization proceeds, the spray lengthens to give space to the slender, two-valved seed-pods.

The flowering period is from May to October.

LADY'S SMOCK

Family CRUCIFERAE *Cardamine pratensis*

In all moist meadows and swampy places the rambler may come across a multitude of waving flowers which look white in the mass but at close quarters are seen to be pale pink or lilac. They are the Lady's Smock, one of our best examples of the Cruciferous plants. The country name in many places is Milkmaids or Cuckoo-flower. Abundant throughout Britain.

The short rootstock sometimes sends off runners and the radical leaves are cut up into a variable number of distinct leaflets more or less rounded, the terminal one being the largest, and as they lie upon the wet ground, root at every leaflet and develop a tiny plant from the axil of each. The stem leaves are longer and narrower. The erect stem, simple or branched, rises to about a foot high terminating in the large flowers, nearly three-quarters of an inch across. The upright slender seed-pod is about an inch long.

The flowering period is from March to June.

FUMITORY

Family FUMARIACEAE   *Fumaria officinalis*

An annual plant common in dry fields and waste places throughout Great Britain. It is a plant that has followed close in the wake of cultivation. Its grace and lightness suggest to the mind some kind of relationship with the Maidenhair - fern, more especially in the lower portion of the plant. The leaves are thin and much divided. It forms a dense tuft a few inches high from which the stem rises to a height of from one to three feet.

The flowers are peculiarly formed and their arrangement is known as a raceme, dense at first but often extending as the flowering advances. They consist of two small sepals and four petals arranged in two unequal pairs ; the upper petal is spurred at the base, the lateral pair connected by their tips and completely enclosing the stamens and pistil and forming a tubular corolla.

It had formerly a great reputation in medicine.

Its flowering period is from May to September.

TREACLE MUSTARD

Family CRUCIFERAE   *Erysimum cheiranthoides*

Not uncommon in the southern half of England, but rare in the northern half and in Ireland, this annual plant is another of the neglected Crucifers that grows in the waste places of fields and roadsides.

It is covered with short, forked hairs which impart a frosted appearance. The stem is straight, round and leafy rising from one to two feet. The leaves are narrow, lance-shaped, scarcely stalked, narrower at the base, and the margins finely toothed.

The small pale-yellow flowers are about a quarter of an inch across ; the petals clawed. The seed-pods are about one inch in length, slender and square ; the valves with a prominent keel, nearly erect.

It is the only British species and closely allied to the Garlic Mustard.

The flowering period is from June to August.

JACK-BY-THE-HEDGE

Family CRUCIFERAE   *Alliaria petiolata*

Known also as Garlic Mustard. It is one of those plentiful hedgerow weeds that are constantly met with.

An annual, it is an erect - growing, fresh-looking plant, though its stems have an inclination to grovel instead of rise. The leaves are more or less heart-shaped, with rounded teeth at the edges, on long stalks of soft texture and hairy beneath. All through the winter these leaves are very conspicuous and attain a large size before the stem begins to rise. It has a strong smell, when bruised, suggestive of garlic.

The flowers are small and white, the four petals arranged crosswise. The seed-pods are about two and a half inches long, slightly curved, the valves being keeled, which gives a four-angled appearance.

In June the caterpillar of the Orange-tip Butterfly may be found feeding upon the pods which they resemble so closely that they are very difficult to distinguish.

It flowers in May and June.

CHARLOCK

Family CRUCIFERAE   *Sinapis arvensis*

Charlock or Wild Mustard is a hairy annual belonging to the cabbage tribe which enjoys the comparatively light and dry soil of the upland cornfield. A pretty sight to the rambler in June amongst the short corn-plants but to the farmer a great nuisance ; for all must be laboriously hand-picked and the land " cleaned " as he would probably express it.

The rough lyre-shaped leaves have boldly-toothed edges with a few smaller leaves on the leaf-stalk, and the stem rises to one or two feet high.

The rather large bright yellow flowers have four petals.

The fruit is an angular pod, with a straight beak, not persistent, and two hairy valves, but containing only one row of dark-brown seeds.

The flowering period is from May to August.

COMMON SCURVY-GRASS

Family CRUCIFERAE   *Cochlearia officinalis*

A biennial or perennial herb, not uncommon on the sea-shores of England and Ireland, more abundant in Scotland and the Highlands.

Several smooth and fleshy stems from four to ten inches high spring from the rootstock ending in a spray of small white four-petalled flowers, each one-third of an inch across.

The radical leaves are more or less heart-shaped, varying to round and kidney-shaped, with long stalks.

The stem leaves are stalkless, clasping the stem, and lobed and toothed.

The seed-pods are nearly round, tipped with a very short style, and the valves are netted.

Scurvy-grass was so called on account of its former prescription as the antidote to the scorbutic troubles of our seafaring folk, who had to rely chiefly upon salted provisions during their lengthy voyages. To-day, those functions are discharged more efficiently by the addition of lime-juice to a more liberal menu.

The flowering period is from May to August.

WOAD

Family CRUCIFERAE   *Isatis tinctoria*

In a few places in the south of England may be found this tall, erect biennial herb. It is regarded as being a long-naturalized waif of former cultivation, but at Tewkesbury, on cliffs by the Severn, it is believed to be truly wild. In former days it was cultivated for the dye its juice produced.

The smooth, stout stem branching towards the top attains a height of two or three feet. Its radical leaves are more or less lance-shaped, with long stalks, whilst its stalkless stem-leaves are shaped more like arrow-heads than lance-heads.

The numerous small yellow flowers are less than a quarter of an inch across and are crowded into erect panicles. The sepals are equal at the base, and the petals equal. The footstalks continue to lengthen after flowering, and curve downwards, so that the oblong seed-pods are all pendulous. These pods are about half an inch long, brown when ripe.

The flowers may be found in July and August.

FIELD PENNY CRESS

Family CRUCIFERAE   *Thlaspi arvense*

In many districts of England it is common in cornfields and roadside wastes, but in the northern kingdom it is not so plentiful.

It is an annual plant, six inches to a foot high, whose first leaves form a rosette upon the ground. Then up springs a slender, un-branched stem, bearing leaves whose general outline is that of an arrow-head, with waved teeth along the margins ; above the leaves are many small white flowers the parts of which are in fours, arranged crosswise. These are succeeded by much larger heart-shaped seed-vessels on long slender stalks which stand out from the stem almost horizontally.

They form a long raceme, the pods about half an inch in diameter, including a very broad wing and deeply notched at the top, with a minute style in the notch.

The plant is also known as Mithridate Mustard. It was regarded by old writers as a valuable anti-dote to poisons.

The flowering period is from May to July.

SHEPHERD'S PURSE

Family CRUCIFERAE   *Capsella bursa-pastoris*

One of the commonest weeds in cultivated and waste places, and one need not travel far to find a specimen, for almost any spot of earth that man has tilled will furnish it, though it has a preference for light soils. An alternative name is Pickpocket.

The tapering rootstock often reaches to a great depth from which rise the pinnately-cut radical leaves. The smaller leaves high on the stem are arrow-shaped with wavy toothed edges. The flowers are white, very minute, without nectar or scent, and are succeeded by the heart-shaped seed-vessel (capsule) which gives its name to the whole plant, from its resemblance to an ancient form of rustic pouch. When ripe the seed-vessel splits into two valves, and the numerous seeds drop out.

In stature the plant varies greatly, according to the position in which it grows—on a gravel path being only two or three inches high, whilst in a garden border it may be almost as many feet.

Flowering throughout the summer.

SEA KALE

Family CRUCIFERAE   *Crambe maritima*

Though found along all the sandy shores of Britain the Sea Kale is really rather a rare plant. Occasionally it may be found away from sand or shingle, as at Beachy Head in Sussex, where it has climbed the great chalk cliffs and established itself.

It has a long, fleshy, burrowing rootstock an inch thick, from which arise spreading stems a foot or two feet long, with splendid oblong heart - shaped leaves, fleshy, and with the margins lobed. The radical leaves, rising from the rootstock, lie along the ground to a length of a couple of feet. On the stout flowering stems, the leaves are much shorter, but much lobed and crisped.

The flowers are borne in great many-branched clusters a foot across ; the individual flower is white with yellow stamens and a purple pistil.

The flowering period extends from May to August.

WILD MIGNONETTE

Family RESEDACEAE   *Reseda lutea*

So familiar is the Sweet Mignonette
of our gardens, and so like and yet
unlike are the wild species, that
whilst no one would take them for
the garden plant, it is easy to see
their natural affinities at a glance.
They are annual herbs, becoming
biennial during mild winters.

It grows in dry, waste places,
especially in chalky districts. Its
leaves vary a great deal but are
pinnate or deeply lobed and much
waved on the margins.

The pale yellow flowers are borne
on a stiff, erect stalk, in a dense
raceme. Individually the flowers
are inconspicuous. The calyx is
irregular, and divided into four to
seven narrow segments ; there is a
similar number of unequal greenish-yellow
petals, each deeply cleft into two lobes, and a
multitude of stamens. The stigmas are lobes at
the mouth of the open ovary. The flowers are
honeyed, though scentless.

The oblong seed capsule is green and opens at
the top long before maturity, each containing
several seeds.

Flowering from June to September.

SEA ROCKET

Family CRUCIFERAE   *Cakile maritima*

An annual to be found on sandy shore or salt-marsh all round our coasts.

The Sea Rocket has a very long tap-root that enables it to draw moisture from the wet depths.

The stem divides early into long, zig-zag branches that may be two feet long and are only half-erect.

The narrow oblong leaves, which are fleshy, have their margins cut into a few blunt lobes. Both branches and leaves have a glaucous " bloom."

The flowers are in small clusters at the end of the branches ; they are about half an inch across, the four petals of a lilac tint, sometimes so pale as to appear white at a distance.

They are succeeded by four-angled seed-pods an inch long, with a sword-shaped tip to the upper of the two joints. There are no valves, and only the upper joint perfects its single seed.

The flowering period is from June to September.

ROCK-ROSE

Family CISTACEAE   *Helianthemum chamaecistus*

Common throughout the country, except in Cornwall and West Scotland, where it is rare. On our southern chalk-downs and on banks in gravelly soils the Rock-rose is abundant. The plant is shrubby and its branches trail on the ground among grass and low herbage.

It is perennial and has a creeping rootstock. The annual flowering branches extend up to nearly a foot long. The leaves are small, oblong, with an even margin ; the upper surface hairy, the lower, downy. They are arranged on the stem in pairs and provided with long slender stipules.

It has only three sepals, but there are two others reduced to the size and shape of stipules. The five somewhat flabby petals have the softness of the poppy.

The open pale-yellow flowers vary from three-quarters to one and a quarter inches across. A multitude of stamens surround the pistil ; they are irritable and on being touched fall back from the pistil.

Flowering from June to September.

47

MILKWORT

*Family P*OLYGALACEAE   *Polygala vulgaris*

Among the grass of heaths, dry pastures and under hedges, the Milkwort may be found. It is profusely distributed in Britain, although it is not a well-known plant. It is only a few inches in height, and scarcely noticeable when not in flower.

It is a perennial with a short, tufted rootstock from which rise numerous stems. The tough, lance-shaped leaves are scattered alternatively on the stem ; crowded somewhat, at the base.

The flower consists of five sepals, the broad inner two of which are coloured purple. The corolla may be of the same hue, or pink, blue, white, or lilac. The stamens cohere, and the corolla is attached to the sheath thus formed, and the pistil has a protecting hood over it.

When the fruit is set the sepals turn *green*. This action appears to have relation to the visits of insects, saving their time by indicating which flowers are still unfertilized.

Flowering from June to August.

48

MAIDEN PINK

Family C*ARYOPHYLLACEAE*   *Dianthus deltoides*

Found in fields and on banks where
the soil is dry. It is a perennial
and is generally distributed from
mid-Scotland southwards. It is
unknown in Ireland except as an
introduced plant.

From its base spring slender
branches about a foot long. The
leaves on the upper part of the
flowering stem are sharply pointed,
lower down the points are blunted,
and on the flowerless shoots they
are strap-shaped.

They are downy and are dis-
posed in pairs, their bases joined.

The flowers are usually solitary,
less than an inch across; calyx
smooth, five-toothed with overlapping bracts below. The petals
not touching, toothed at their edges; of a beautiful rosy colour, dotted with white. The flower
is without scent, but it secretes nectar which is
produced by a fleshy yellow gland at the bottom
of the corolla tube, so that only long-tongued
insects can reach it. There are ten stamens and
two long styles with curled stigmas.

The flowering period extends from June to
September.

SWEET VIOLET

Family VIOLACEAE   *Viola odorata*

Found truly wild only in the south and east of England, and possibly the east of Ireland ; but it is naturalized in many other parts of the kingdom. It may be found on banks, under hedges, in woods and on the borders of meadows.

It is justly one of our most valued flowers of spring.

It has a short rootstock which gives off runners. From the rootstock spring the long-stemmed leaves. They are broadly heart-shaped and have a way of enlarging greatly after the plant has flowered.

The sweet-scented flowers vary in colour ; they may be blue, reddish-purple, or white. The petals are unequal in size and shape, there being two pairs and an odd one. This is larger than the others and is produced backwards as a short hollow spur. It is really the uppermost of the five petals, but, owing to the flower-stalk invariably bending over near the summit, it appears to us always as the lowest.

Flowering from March to May.

WILD PANSY

The Wild Pansy will be found on hilly pastures, in cultivated fields and waste places generally.

Branching stems rise from the rootstock, the large leaf-like stipules deeply divided into several lobes, the terminal one the largest. The leaves, too, assume forms very different from those of the typical species. It differs, also, from all other species of *Viola* in the fact that the two upper petals of the flower are very erect instead of leaning forward.

The flowers vary from white, through yellow to purple, or there may be a mixture of two or more of these tints. The two upper pairs of petals slightly overlap each other and are usually more coloured, the lower petals always broadest and generally yellow at the base.

The flowering period extends from May to September.

COMMON PEARLWORT

Family CARYOPHYLLACEAE   *Sagina procumbens*

The Common Pearlwort will be found in all sorts of waste places, pastures and banks. The Pearlworts are among the smallest of our flowering plants. Owing to the minuteness of their parts it is not an easy matter to discriminate between the recognized species.

Although *Sagina procumbens* is a type common throughout the country, few people know it by its name.

It is a perennial that forms a low tuft or mat by means of a number of trailing and rooting branches.

The leaves are awl-shaped, in pairs and united at their base, ending in a fine hair-like point.

The numerous small flowers are borne singly on separate delicate stalks and the parts usually in fours, occasionally fives ; four sepals, four much smaller white petals (sometimes wanting), four stamens and four curved styles.

After pollination the tip of the stalk curves, so that the flower hangs downwards ; but straightens again when the seed-capsule is ripe.

Flowers may be found from May to September.

SEA SANDWORT

Family CARYOPHYLLACEAE   *Honkenya peploides*

All around our islands, wherever the shore is sandy or pebbly, this common perennial often forms extensive carpets, rendered somewhat conspicuous by the dark, shining green colour of the fleshy leaves and stems.

It has a creeping rootstock from which emerge forking stems that lie on the ground, whilst their branches rise to a height of only six or eight inches.

The oval leaves have horny margins, are stalkless and arranged in pairs, each pair is at right-angles with those next above and below, their tips curved back.

The small greenish-white flowers which expand only in the morning sunshine, and which may be solitary or two or three together, have short stalks arising from the axils of the leaves. The complete bisexual flower has five blunt oval sepals, five petals, ten stamens alternately long and short, and the pistil has three or five styles.

The large round seed-vessels contain only a few large, black, pear-shaped seeds.

Flowering from May to September.

BLADDER CAMPION

Family CARYOPHYLLACEAE   *Silene vulgaris*

A perennial plant frequently to be found on roadside wastes and on the margins of cornfields. It belongs to a group familiarly known as Catch-flies, owing to certain species being coated with short sticky hairs, to which green-fly and other small insects adhere with fatal results.

From a stout rootstock, erect branching stems rise to two or three feet. The round, slim stem gives off a pair of pointed leaves, from enlarged joints.

The white flowers are all slightly drooping, in loose terminal panicles. The sepals are united to form a swollen bladdery-looking calyx of grey-green colour, with a darker network of nerves. The mouth of the bladder is cut into five teeth, to indicate the sepals of which it is composed. The five petals are each deeply cloven into two narrow segments, and just below the cleft there are two scarcely noticeable scales. There are ten stamens but the number of styles varies from three to five.

Flowering from June to September.

RED CAMPION

Family CARYOPHYLLACEAE

Silene dioica

To be found in moist, shady places, woods and hedge-banks.

It is a perennial. The root-leaves are egg-shaped, but those on the stem are much narrower. The hairy stems, up to three feet high, forking repeatedly above, and towards their extremity, becoming glandular.

The scentless flowers consist of the dark red calyx, and the rosy-pink petals. The broad portion of the petal is cleft into two lobes, and where it narrows to the claw there are a couple of little scales that are erect. The flowers are—in botanical language—*diœcious*. In some we find stamens, but the pistil with its five stigmas is absent or undeveloped ; in others the reverse is the case ; and this arrangement necessitates the agency of insects in the transfer of pollen from staminate flowers to those with pistils. The result is the development of the ovary into an egg-shaped capsule, which splits at its smaller end to liberate the ripened seeds.

Flowering from June to September.

GREATER STITCHWORT

Family CARYOPHYLLACEAE   *Stellaria holostea*

In hedges, open woods and bushy places may be found the Greater Stitchwort.

It is a perennial, with a creeping rootstock. The erect, though weak, four-angled stems rise early in the year. As the thin stems elongate they lean against the other constituents of the hedgerow for support.

The long, narrow, rigid, sharp-pointed leaves are arranged in pairs, which are more or less connected at their bases.

The numerous star-like white flowers are produced in panicles of a few flowers only. They consist of five sepals, five petals which are much longer than the sepals and cleft almost to the middle. There are ten stamens and three styles. Five of the stamens elevate themselves so that the anthers come out of the tube and discharge their pollen. That pollen is produced for the good of the species, for it can be of no use to the flower that produced it. When carried by some insect, it serves to fertilize another flower.

Flowering April to June.

SALTMARSH SAND-SPURREY

Family CARYOPHYLLACEAE   *Spergularia media*

A not very common perennial to be found in muddy salt-marshes. Low growing and prostrate it has a woody root-stock from which rise the flattened trailing stems, usually smooth. The fleshy narrow leaves are half-round in section, but have blunt tips. The stipules are broadly triangular. The five pale lilac or nearly white petals are equal in length to, or slightly less than the sepals. There are ten stamens and three, sometimes four or five, styles. The seed-capsule is one and a half to twice the length of the sepals, and the reddish seeds have a broad wing.

It will be found in flower all the summer.

RAGGED ROBIN

Family CARYOPHYLLACEAE   *Lychnis flos-cuculi*

The Ragged Robin may be found in moist places, whether wet meadow, ditch or bog.

It is a perennial with a short rootstock from which its stem rises to a height of two feet, and is reddish, the upper part rough and sticky.

The lance-shaped leaves that spring directly from the slender rootstock are stalked; the more slender ones on the reddish stem are not.

The flowers are borne on loose terminal panicles, red and without scent. The calyx is dark red, with purple veins, and the petals are rosy in colour and cut into four toothed narrow segments, of which the two inner ones are very long, so that the extreme diameter of the flower is about one and a quarter inches. Occasionally the flowers may be found with undivided petals, and rarely the flowers are white.

The flowers produce nectar, and the stamens come to maturity before the stigmas, thus favouring cross-fertilization.

The flowering period is from May to August.

CORN COCKLE

Family CARYOPHYLLACEAE Agrostemma githago

Wandering through or round our cornfields any time during summer, one is almost sure to find this beautiful flower.

It is an annual, tall and erect, the stems clothed with white hairs, and attaining a height of four or five feet.

The leaves are long and narrow, four or five inches long, and not unlike the leaves of the corn-plants surrounding them.

The flowers are solitary, of a rich purple within, much paler without, and measure nearly two inches across. The woolly calyx is in one, strongly ribbed, with five very long leaf-like teeth, that considerably exceed the petals in length.

The flowers produce nectar, but owing to the length of the tube it is only accessible to the long tongues of butterflies and moths, who are instrumental in effecting its cross-fertilization.

This is the only native species.

The flowering period is from June to September.

CORN SPURREY

Family CARYOPHYLLACEAE   *Spergula arvensis*

The Corn Spurrey will be found in cornfields, on dry soils, when the corn has not grown too high to prevent one from seeing between the ranks.

It is an annual, and the straggling downy stems rise branching from the root, attaining a height of one or two feet, with bent joints.

The leaves are half-round, awl-shaped, very slender, in distant pairs, and springing from their axils, give the appearance of whorls.

The minute white flowers are gathered into cymes at the ends of the stems, and have foot-stalks of varying lengths, which bring them all to the same level, on the principle of the umbel, but the umbel likeness is not very complete owing to those flowers which have set their seeds bending down by the depression of their footstalks. The five sepals are oval. Petals five. Stamens ten, with roundish anthers; ovary egg-shaped with five curved styles.

Flowering from June to August.

COMMON FLAX

Family LINACEAE   *Linum usitatissimum*

Wherever the Common Flax is found, it will be an escape from cultivation, which readily sows itself as a weed. As a truly wild plant the "most used" flax is not known, but in cultivation, as the parent of linen garments, it has been known from the infancy of the human race. To-day the exports of flax and linen from Great Britain are worth many millions of pounds per annum. It is therefore a plant that would be entitled to respectful consideration when we meet it.

It is an annual plant with erect, slender stems extending to about one and a half feet high.

Its narrow lance-shaped leaves are arranged alternately and at a distance from each other.

The flowers are large, and purplish-blue in colour, borne in a loose terminal corymb. Five is the number dominating the structure of the flower ; sepals, petals, stamens, glands, ovary (five cells), styles—all fives.

The flowering period is in June and July.

COMMON MOUSE-EAR CHICKWEED

Family CARYOPHYLLACEAE *Cerastium holosteoides*

In all kinds of waste places, pastures and woods, wet or dry, this plant may be found.

From the root the spreading stems rise, with straight joints, and thickening where they connect. At the joints, called *nodes*, the stalkless leaves are given off in pairs whose bases almost join, and between them encircle the stem.

The flowers are white and are gathered all together at the summit of the stem in clusters called *cymes*, where they ripen in pairs, the footstalk lengthening until it is much longer than the five hairy sepals. Within, there is a central disk, upon which five glands secrete nectar for the benefit of fertilizing insects ; and it also supports the stamens, and the curved cylindrical ovary, surmounted in turn by five branched stigmas.

The seed-capsule opens at the top by splitting into ten teeth and allowing the dark seeds to escape.

It flowers principally from April to August, but its blossoms may be found throughout the autumn.

RED SAND-SPURREY

Family CARYOPHYLLACEAE *Spergularia rubra*

Although common and widely distributed in this country, Sand-Spurrey is by no means a well-known plant. It should be looked for in gravelly soils, about salt-marshes, and in the crevices of seaside rocks.

From its woody root-stock a great number of slender ruddy stems start off, but remain almost prostrate.

The leaves grow in little bunches at the joints, surrounded by semi-transparent silvery stipules ; each leaf in the bunch being of different size from the others, almost cylindrical, thicker towards the free end, and bluntly pointed.

The upper portions of the stems, also the sepals, are covered with short hairs.

There are five sepals of a ruddy-green colour. The five petals are of a bright rosy tint, the under-surface paler. Stamens ten, the anthers bright yellow. Stigmas three. When the flower has faded, its short stalk hangs down, but when the seeds are ripe, the stalk again becomes erect.

Flowering from June to September.

TREE MALLOW

Family MALVACEAE   *Lavatera arborea*

Along the south and west coasts of England, and in the Firth of Forth, but rarely on the Irish coast, this plant may be found growing from crevices in the rocks. It is much more rare generally, than it was formerly.

It has an erect, branching, woody stem, rising from three to six feet high, and three or four inches thick.

The leaves are large, long-stalked and velvety, and roundish in general outline. They are cut into five or seven lobes with rounded teeth ; they are also plaited, the folds running from the stalk along the middle of each lobe and a reverse fold to the indent between the lobes. From the axils of the leaves are produced annual flowering shoots bearing numerous blossoms.

The flowers are an inch and a half across, the outer calyx (epicalyx) having three large oval lobes. The glossy petals are rosy purple, veined with darker purple.

The fruits form a ring of one-seeded carpels.

Flowering from July to September.

MARSH MALLOW

Family MALVACEAE *Althaea officinalis*

The Marsh Mallow is a perennial of only local occurrence, to be found in marshes near the sea, chiefly in England and Ireland ; rare in Scotland and then always south of the Clyde.

The simple or slightly branched stems are from two to three feet high. The large, thick leaves are oval heart-shaped, divided into three or five lobes, which have coarsely - toothed edges. The stems, leaves and inflorescence are covered with a soft, velvety down.

The pale rose flowers are produced in small clusters from the axils of the stem-leaves. The outer calyx (epicalyx) has from six to nine divisions. There are five lobes to the calyx, five petals attached to a tube consisting of the connected filaments of the many stamens. Through this tube protrude the numerous styles. The fruits form a ring of one-seeded carpels.

Marsh Mallow has undoubted demulcent properties to the irritated mucous membrane ; but formerly it was considered to have far more extensive curative powers.

The flowering period is during August and September.

TAMARISK

Family TAMARICACEAE   *Tamarix gallica*

The Tamarisk will be constantly met with at seaside places on the south, east and west of England.

It is a small tree or bush, reaching ten or twelve feet high, with pliant, feathery branches and minute evergreen leaves, which are triangular with keeled backs and eared bases, closely overlapping and appearing to be mere scales. It is not a native, but having been grown in southern England for so long, it is now considered as an indigene. Its great recommendation is the power to withstand cutting salt winds, and as it is readily propagated by cuttings, it has become extensively used as protective hedges for seaside gardens in the localities referred to.

Its flowers are minute, white or pink, clustered in a blunt spike about one and a half inches long. They consist of four or five lance-shaped sepals, five petals and a tapering ovary, with three or four short styles.

The fruit is triangular in section.

It flowers from July to as late as November in mild districts.

PERFORATED ST. JOHN'S WORT

Family HYPERICACEAE   *Hypericum perforatum*

Common in copse, on hedgebank and roadside throughout the country, as far north as Sutherland.

From a perennial rootstock, with short runners or barren shoots, rise the very erect two-edged stems, pale brown and smooth, to a height of two or three feet, branching in the upper part.

The oblong leaves are clean-cut without stalks. If the leaves are held up to the light it will be found that the veins (but not the reticulations) are pellucid and that the leaf is thickly dotted with pellucid glands.

The bright yellow flowers are in cymose clusters, with a multitude of stamens, which are more or less joined, in three bundles. The flowers are one to one and a quarter inches in diameter. The calyx and corolla are more or less marked with black dots and lines. There are five pointed sepals and five petals which are twice as long. Ovary large, pear-shaped, surmounted by three long styles. Sepals glandular.

Flowering from July to September.

DOVE'S-FOOT CRANE'S-BILL

Family GERANIACEAE   *Geranium molle*

This neat member of a charming family is a familiar plant of the wayside and pasture.

It is an annual, and from a tough rootstock forms a tuft, more or less hairy The stems are weak and spreading, and swollen at the joints, very short when first flowering.

The leaf-stalks are long, and the numerous radical leaves, though their general outline is kidney-shaped, are deeply cut into about seven lobes, which are in turn lobed and toothed. The upper leaves are fewer and smaller.

The rosy flowers are borne in pairs, on a short peduncle, the sepals are scarcely pointed, and the broader end of the petal is notched in the middle, and the narrow lower portion is fringed with hairs.

The carpels, or divisions of the seed-vessel, are keeled but not wrinkled, and the seeds are pitted.

The flowering period is from May to September.

HEMLOCK STORK'S-BILL

Family GERANIACEAE   *Erodium cicutarium*

To be found on cultivated lands and dry pastures, especially near the coast.

It is an annual. From a thick tap-root it often forms a dense tuft, from which the short stems extend. The pinnate leaves are cut up into a large number of leaflets, arranged in slightly irregular pairs on either side of the rib, and these leaflets are again cut up into many irregular lobes.

The pink flowers are borne in the form of umbels, consisting of from two to twelve flowers, and comprise five sepals, five petals, ten stamens (five of which are imperfect) and five stigmas.

The tails of the carpels are lined with silky hairs, they twist spirally, causing the hairs to stand out at right-angles. The seed remains attached to the tail, which becomes detached from the axis of the style and falls to the ground. There the twisted tail is alternately lengthened and shortened by moisture and dryness, and this movement gradually forces the seed into the ground.

Flowering from June to September.

COMMON MALLOW

Family MALVACEAE   *Malva sylvestris*

A plant of considerable beauty which may be found in field, copse or roadside.

It is a biennial or perennial with an erect, hairy stem, growing to a height of three or four feet. The leaves, on long stalks, are kidney-shaped, the margins broken up into five lobes which have toothed edges.

The large, pale purple flowers, with darker lines converging to the centre, are produced from the axils of the leaves, and are about one and a half inches in diameter. The five petals are heart-shaped. In newly-opened flowers it will be noticed that the anthers ripen and shed their pollen before the ten styles are mature. When, later, the stigmatic upper surfaces of these become fit for pollination, they hold themselves above the drooping stamens, so that self-fertilization is impossible.

The fruits consist of a number of one-seeded carpels, arranged in a ring.

Flowering from June to September.

WOOD SORREL

Family GERANIACEAE *Oxalis acetosella*

One of the most graceful and charming of our native plants. It abounds in moist, shady woods. A favourite position for it is the rotten centre of some old beech stump from which it will spread in a loose cluster, or growing on the ground, often in great abundance.

The roots are fine and scattered along the creeping knotted pink stems. The leaflets, fresh yellow-green trefoils, backed with purple, droop close to the stalk at night or on the approach of rain, contracting or expanding under the influence of darkness or light respectively. The leaves have a pleasant acid flavour due to oxalic acid.

The white flowers, streaked with pink, are large and are borne on long and slender radical stems, and consist of five sepals, five petals, ten stamens and five stigmas.

The fruit is a five-angled irritable capsule, from which the black seeds are thrown with great force, up to a distance of several yards.

Flowering April and May.

BROOM

Family LEGUMINOSAE   *Sarothamnus scoparius*

A shrub, three to five feet high, which may be found on hilly downs, bushy places and wastes. Often confounded with the Furze, by the non-botanical rambler, due, no doubt, to the similarity of the flowers, and the partiality of both for heaths and commons. The principal difference between the two is, that whilst the Furze has sharp spines instead of ordinary leaves, the Broom rarely puts on any prickles at all.

It has numerous long, erect green branches and has compound leaves, of three small leaflets.

The large, bright yellow flowers are solitary or in pairs, on slender stalks springing from the axils of the old leaves. The calyx is two-lipped and there are five petals, a large upper petal, two lateral ones, and a lower pair which are united, forming a boat-shaped body. Within this body lie the stamens and pistil, and the former have the filaments united into a tube within which lies the ovary.

Flowering from April to June.

LUCERNE

Family LEGUMINOSAE   *Medicago sativa*

Though this handsome plant will be found growing apparently wild in the hedgerow and on the borders of fields, it must not be hastily concluded to be a native. The species is largely grown in this country as a green fodder plant, for which it is highly esteemed, and it has escaped from the fields and reproduced itself without man's aid.

The rootstock is perennial and the branched stems are hollow. The oblong leaves are trifoliate, with long-pointed and toothed stipules at the base of the leaf-stalk.

The deep purple (sometimes yellow) flowers are crowded at the top of the long stalks, which rise from the axils of the leaves.

A peculiarity of this genus consists in the downy seed-pod being more or less spirally twisted, so as to form two or sometimes three complete rings or coils.

The flowering period is from May to July.

FURZE

Family LEGUMINOSAE   *Ulex europaeus*

Abundant in England, Ireland and southern Scotland, on heaths and sandy places. It is about April that it is in its full glory, and one may gather, about that time, enormous trusses of deliciously fragrant golden flowers—if one is not deterred by its formidable spines.

It is a shrub, growing as high as six feet, and more or less hairy. The numerous short branches, from which the flowers spring, all terminate in a stout, very sharp thorn.

The calyx is divided into two parts only, is large and thin, minutely toothed, and coloured yellow, which is subdued by the black hairs that cover it. There are large bracts below the flowers.

The black hairy seed-pod is but slightly longer than the calyx, the valves elastic, which causes them, when ripe, to curl up with a crackling noise, and scatter widely the polished seeds.

As a seedling, the Furze has soft hairy leaves that are trefoils ; but as the plant grows older the new leaf material is produced as spines.

NEEDLE-WHIN

Family LEGUMINOSAE   *Genista anglica*

Known also as Needle-furze this prickly, shrubby plant may be found on heaths, moors and bushy pastures in England and the greater part of Scotland.

The slender, woody branches spread in all directions, covered with spines and minute lance-shaped leaves. The spines vary from a half to one inch in length, and occasionally will be found branched.

The yellow flowers, which spring from the axils of the bract-leaves, are about half an inch long, have short footstalks, and are of the usual Pea type of structure.

The calyx is two-lipped, the upper one cut into two lobes, the lower shorter, with three short triangular teeth.

The filaments of the stamens are all united to form a tube, and the anthers are alternately long and short

The seed-pod is broad and much inflated, about three-quarters of an inch long, and pointed at each end.

Flowering in May and June.

BIRD'S-FOOT TREFOIL

Family LEGUMINOSAE   *Lotus corniculatus*

From June to October our commons, pastures and downs are bright with the flowers of Bird's-foot Trefoil. It is known in some districts as Lady's Slipper.

From a short, woody, perennial rootstock, several trailing branches originate, which are themselves much branched. The leaves are not trefoils, as the name would lead one to suppose, for the apparent stipules at the base of the leaf-stalk are, in this genus, leaflets.

The flowers, which are in spreading heads of from three to ten flowers, are of bright yellow, tinted with red.

They are succeeded by little cylindrical pods about one inch in length, which, when three or four are in a cluster, present the appearance of a bird's claw.

The seeds are globular, separated by a pithy substance, which nearly fills the pod.

The plant is a valued ingredient in the formation of pastures and meadows.

HARE'S-FOOT TREFOIL

Family LEGUMINOSAE   *Trifolium arvense*

To be found in cornfields, dry pastures or on sandy banks. The Hare's-foot may be taken as the type of a small and distinct group of Clovers, with the flower-heads of cylindrical form.

It is a downy annual, growing to about a foot high, and its general appearance is delicate and pretty.

The many, almost erect branching stems are clothed with short hairs and have rather distant leaves of three slender leaflets, a half to three-quarters of an inch long. The leaf-stalk is provided with a pair of large stipules ending in long bristly points.

The pinky-white flowers are very small and numerous, gathered in very soft and feathery heads, a half to one inch long, on lengthening stalks. The bristly appearance of the flower-heads is due to the fine hairy teeth of the calyx projecting beyond the small corolla.

The flowering period is from July to September.

REST-HARROW

The Rest-Harrow will be found in barren pastures and ill-cultivated fields. Known in Sussex and Hampshire as the Cammock, the Rest-Harrow or Wrest-Harrow, it is one of those plants whose presence in the pasture is said to indicate poverty or neglect.

It is a perennial low shrub, sometimes creeping near the ground, and at others growing more erect.

The rootstock often creeps underground, and is particularly tough. The plant is often spiny, and reaches a height of a foot or more. The leaflets are oblong.

The flowers are similar in structure to those of Broom, and may be borne either singly or in racemes. They are pink in colour ; the petal, known as the standard, is very large in this species, and streaked with a red of a deeper shade. The flower does not secrete nectar, and the insect visitors only obtain pollen for their trouble.

The seed-pod is very small, containing two or three seeds.

The flowering period is from June to September.

TALL MELILOT

Family LEGUMINOSAE   *Melilotus altissima*

In field corners, bushy hedgerows, and roadside wastes the rambler may come across one of the Melilots. Of the three species found in this country, two have yellow flowers ; and until they have ripened their seed-pods it is difficult to say whether you have the native *M. altissima* or the alien *M. officinalis*. If the two could be examined side by side it would be seen that the flowers of the Tall Melilot are of a deeper yellow than the other.

The Tall Melilot is three or four feet high, with distant, long-stalked leaves broken up into three slender, oval leaflets with toothed edges. At the base of the stalk there is a pair of bristle-like stipules. From the axils of the leaf-stalk stand out the long, flowering branches, bearing many flowers, all drooping in one direction. The petals are all of the same length.

The hairy seed-pod has net-like markings and, when ripe, is black.

Flowering from June to August.

HORSESHOE VETCH

Family LEGUMINOSAE   *Hippocrepis comosa*

May be found on chalk hills and stony pastures, but only in England, and in Ayr and Kincardine. It does not occur in Ireland. On the North Downs in Surrey it will be met with in great profusion.

It is a perennial plant with a woody rootstock from which rise many branching stems, either short or spreading along the ground, six inches to a foot long.

The leaves are pinnate, though the leaflets are not so numerous. They vary from four to eight pairs, with an odd one at the tip, the lowest pair at a distance from the stem.

The yellow flowers are borne at the top of the curved flower-stalks, in the form of umbels, each umbel consisting of from six to ten blossoms.

They are succeeded by rough, jointed seedpods, serpentine in shape, about an inch long, ending in a fine point.

The flowering period is from May to August.

SAINFOIN

Family LEGUMINOSAE   *Onobrychis viciifolia*

A handsome herb, much cultivated as a fodder plant in dry
fields, but will also be found
growing wild on chalk-hills and
downs.

It is perennial and from a
woody rootstock spring its
more or less erect downy stems,
one to one and a half feet high.

The leaves are pinnate, the
leaflets in about twelve pairs
and a terminal one.

The bright, clear pink
flowers, veined with a deeper
rosy tint, and with a broad
standard petal, form a more or
less closely packed spike.

The seed-pod, about an inch
long, and ending in a fine
point, is semi-circular, wrinkled and contains but
one seed.

Sain-foin is a word borrowed from the French
and means, literally, *wholesome-hay* or fodder.

The flowering period is from June to August.

RED CLOVER

Family LEGUMINOSAE   *Trifolium pratense*

In meadows, pastures and by the roadsides the Common Red or Purple Clover may generally be found in the wild state. It has, however, been so long cultivated as a valuable fodder plant that in some localities it may not be truly indigenous.

It has a perennial stock, but of few years' duration, from which rise the hairy, nearly erect stems, one to two feet long. Its large, oval leaflets are frequently marked with a whitish band, that takes, more or less, a quarter-moon shape.

The purplish-red flowers are composed of dense, globular heads, afterwards becoming longer than broad, with two trifoliate leaves close to their base. The calyx teeth are slender and bristly, not longer than the corolla. After flowering the petals turn brown, and when the seed is set the petals do not fall off, but simply dry up and wrap themselves around the seed-pod.

The flowering period extends from May to September.

HOP TREFOIL

Family LEGUMINOSAE   *Trifolium campestre*

An annual. To be found in dry pastures, meadows and by the roadsides. Abundant in Britain generally but rare in northern Scotland.

From the rootstock rise the much-branched stems. They are downy, one growing nearly erect, from six inches to a foot long, others all round it are creeping. The trefoil leaflets are oval, the small end near the base, the central one some little distance from the others.

The flowers are pale yellow, thirty to fifty of them, gathered together in a loosely globular head, and are supported on rather long stalks, springing from the axils of the leaves. In fading, the flowers become reflexed and the broad upper petal arching over the *straight* pod, turning bright brown, giving the head the appearance of a hop strobile. In this species the small one-seeded pods are always so covered.

The flowering period is from June to August.

TUFTED VETCH

Family LEGUMINOSAE   *Vicia cracca*

In hedges and bushy places, throughout the summer the bright blue flower-clusters of the Tufted Vetch may be seen.

It is a perennial, with a creeping rootstock, with weak annual stems rising to a length of two to four feet. It climbs by means of the branched tendrils at the ends of the leaf-stalks. The leaves are pinnate, with many narrow, oblong leaflets. They vary in size and may be as much as four inches long.

The flowers are numerous, varying from ten to thirty, all directed to one side of the raceme, which has a stalk several inches in length, though the footstalks of the individual flowers are very short. The flowers themselves are about half an inch long, bright blue, and hanging, somewhat, by their footstalks.

They are succeeded by a flattened, beaked seed-pod, an inch or less in length and containing six or eight seeds.

The flowering period extends from June to August or September.

BUSH VETCH

Family LEGUMINOSAE *Vicia sepium*

In hedges, woods, and bushy places the Bush Vetch will frequently be found.

It is a slightly hairy perennial and has a creeping rootstock, which gives off numerous runners, so that an old plant forms great masses. Its weak and straggling stems grow to a length of one to two feet.

The leaves consist of six to eight pairs of oval leaflets, which vary in different individuals, in some having a squarish end, in others tapering shortly.

The leaf-stalk ends in a tendril, usually branched.

The stipules are half arrow-shaped.

The flowers are pale purple, and are produced in clusters of four to six, on short stems, from the axils of the leaves. The style has a dense tuft of hairs under the stigma on the outer side, with a few short hairs on the opposite side.

The smooth, blackish seed-pod is about an inch long, with a beak, and contains about eight seeds.

Flowering from June to September.

KIDNEY VETCH

Family LEGUMINOSAE   *Anthyllis vulneraria*

Will be found in hilly districts chiefly, in dry pastures or on rocky banks.

It is a perennial and from a woody rootstock rise several stems up to a foot long, and a large number of radical leaves, the whole plant, more or less, clothed with short, silky hairs. The leaves from the stems (cauline leaves) have a number of leaflets in pairs, as well as a terminal one.

The flowers are borne in heads, with an involucre of leaflets, and the heads are chiefly in pairs. The calyx is membranous, and therefore permanent, the mouth oblique, with five teeth. The petals are nearly equal in length, and typically yellow, but subject to considerable variation. In some coast localities the flowers may be found white, cream-coloured, crimson or purple. After flowering the straw-coloured calyx becomes inflated, and the roundish, smooth and veined pod, with its solitary seed, is hidden within.

It is ordinarily in flower from June to August.

YELLOW PEA

Family LEGUMINOSAE   *Lathyrus pratensis*

Known also as the Meadow
Vetchling, this plant is
fairly common in moist
meadow and copse, and
on hedge-banks throughout
Britain.

It is a perennial, with
weak, much branched
stems, straggling to the
length of one or two feet.

It has a creeping under-
ground rootstock, from
which rise several sharp-
angled stems. The leaves
are each divided into two
lance-shaped leaflets, with,
in most cases, a short
branched tendril springing

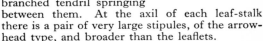

between them. At the axil of each leaf-stalk
there is a pair of very large stipules, of the arrow-
head type, and broader than the leaflets.

From six to ten small, bright yellow flowers are
borne in racemes, supported by a stalk, an inch
or more in length. The calyx is tubular, with
five long awl-shaped points, and the large erect
petal, called the standard, is marked with several
thin purple streaks. The style is flattened and
its inner surface bearded.

It may be found in flower from June to September.

GRASS PEA

In bushy places, grassy borders of fields, the Grass Pea, *in bloom*, may be looked for, as, until the flowers are out, it would be almost useless to search for it, as it is got up to resemble a grass plant exactly.

It is an annual plant, with an erect stem branching from the base, and growing to a height of about two feet, and is entirely without true leaves, leaflets or tendrils. The leaf-stalk, however, is flattened out until it closely resembles a blade of grass ending in a fine point, and the stipules at its base greatly help the deception.

The flowers, which are crimson in colour, are rather small, solitary, and borne on a very long footstalk. They have the power of self-pollination.

The flowers are succeeded by long, slender, straight pods, which are at first very flat, but become cylindrical when the contained peas are fully developed.

Flowering in June and July.

88

WOOD AVENS

Family ROSACEAE   *Geum urbanum*

On the borders of woods, in copses, and on shady hedgebanks, the Avens is abundant.

It is a perennial, with a short, creeping rootstock, from which spring the radical leaves, the blade of which is broken up into distinct lobes and toothed leaflets, widely separated, and varying in size and shape, the terminal leaflet very large, the lowest ones very small. The stipules are large and leafy.

The flowering-stem may reach a length of three feet, bearing erect, solitary, bright yellow flowers on long branching footstalks. The calyx has five long, pointed lobes, with five pointed bracts. The five petals spread themselves out flat, the calyx lobes showing green between them. The crowd of stamens may not easily be numbered; the carpels, too, are numerous, and develop into a head of nutlets, each with a sharp, curved hook at its tip, by which they catch in fur and feather, and so get distributed by bird and beast.

Flowering chiefly between June and August.

Family ROSACEAE   *Filipendula ulmaria*

Known also as Queen of the Meadows, it will be found in wet meadows, and by the sides of streams and rivers.

It has a short, perennial rootstock, with erect, rather stout, reddish stems, two or three feet high. The leaves are interruptedly pinnate, the terminal leaflet three-lobed, the undersides being downy and white. The stem leaves are provided with broad-toothed stipules.

The minute yellowish - white sweetly-scented flowers are very numerous and are borne in large, dense cymes at the summit of the stems. The calyx has four or five lobes ; the petals are four or five, the capsules vary from five to nine, curiously twisted, and surrounded by a large number of stamens.

In spite of their delicate fragrance, the flowers produce no nectar ; but attracted by their sweet odour, insects visit them in great numbers, and from the closeness of the flowers cannot help fertilizing them.

The flowering period extends from June to August.

BRAMBLE

Family ROSACEAE   *Rubus fruticosus*

In hedges, thickets and waste places, the Bramble abounds everywhere.

It has a perennial rootstock from which spring the thick stems. They are provided with hooks, prickles and gland-tipped hairs, all variously intermingled. Growing half-erect to a great length, the stem then arches over until the tip touches the earth, when roots are formed and a new plant arises.

The leaves are compound, usually with three or five oval leaflets, arranged pinnately, and more or less downy. The midribs and stalks are usually armed with hooked prickles.

The white or pink flowers are in panicles at the end of the branches. The calyx forms a broad tube with five lobes ; petals five and stamens many. The numerous carpels are grouped upon a conical receptacle, each containing two ovules, of which only one develops into a seed.

The fruit is a black or purple drupe, but very minute and stalkless, a large number being clustered together on the receptacle to form the so-called Blackberry.

Flowering from June to September.

BARREN STRAWBERRY

Family ROSACEAE *Potentilla sterilis*

To be found on banks, dry pastures and in open woods, the Barren Strawberry is one of the earliest of the flowering plants to make its presence known.

It is often mistaken by the rambler for the true Wild Strawberry, owing to the close resemblance of leaf and flower.

The Barren Strawberry has a branching rootstock, with a tuft of *silky* radical leaves and hairy stalks, *without* the deeply sunken nerve lines of the leaf and the long runners, with young plants attached, of the Wild Strawberry ; but when the fruit is formed there is no difficulty in distinguishing one from the other.

The leaves consist of three leaflets, regularly toothed almost all round. The white flowers are supported on somewhat erect hairy stems, with five small notched petals, narrow and scarcely as long as the calyx.

The receptacle does not swell and become juicy and red as in the Wild Strawberry, but is a barren counterfeit of a mere cluster of dry achenes.

Flowering in early spring.

SILVERWEED

Family ROSACEAE   *Potentilla anserina*

Although this is a common roadside weed, it may also be found growing abundantly and much more luxuriantly in wet pastures.

Its rootstock is the centre from which many rooting runners radiate, sending up its long, pinnate leaves, which show the silvery whiteness of the underside caused by the silky down with which they are covered. The deeply-toothed leaflets are not opposite, but alternate ; and there is the very peculiar arrangement of a miniature leaflet being placed between each two large ones. This form is known as *imparipinnate*.

The solitary yellow flower, large in proportion to the plant, is borne singly on a long stalk, rising from the axil of the leaf. The calyx is cleft into five lobes, which alternate with five longer and divided bracteoles. There are five petals and many stamens and carpels.

It flowers chiefly from June to August, and sparingly much later in the year.

WILD STRAWBERRY

Family ROSACEAE *Fragaria vesca*

Wherever there are shady banks and woodland clearings, this charming little plant is sure to be met with.

It has a perennial, woody rootstock clothed in silky hairs, from which rise three or four trefoil leaves, and a runner or two starting off to produce young plants.

The hairy leaflets are oblong with edges cut into coarse teeth, and showing strongly marked lines on the surface.

The white flowers are borne on the radical, erect flower-stem, and are about three-quarters of an inch across, the lobes of the calyx showing between the five petals. There is an epicalyx of five bracteoles, which are slightly smaller than the calyx lobes. There are ten stamens and numerous pistils.

After fertilization, the receptacle gradually enlarges to such a size that the achenes, formerly packed close together, become widely separated.

The so-called berry becomes red as it ripens, and its tissues are filled with sweet juices.

Flowering nearly the whole summer.

CINQUEFOIL

Family ROSACEAE   *Potentilla reptans*

On grasslands and roadside wastes one may be sure to find the neat leaves and long, slender, creeping stems of the Cinquefoil.

It has woody rootstocks, which extend for a foot or more in the soil, black outside and red within, and at their upper end these branch and form several crowns. From each of these crowns, run off, in all directions, slender stems, yards in length, rooting frequently to peg themselves down, and clothed at intervals with long-stalked leaves. These leaves are broken up into five toothed and egg-shaped leaflets, arranged finger-fashion (*digitate*).

The golden-yellow flowers are about an inch across and arise singly on slender stalks from the axils of the leaves. The five petals alternate with the green sepals, which show between them. Below the sepals there is a set of little bracts (*bracteoles*), collectively spoken of as the *epicalyx* The stamens and pistils ripen simultaneously.

Flowering from June to September.

LADY'S MANTLE

Family ROSACEAE   *Alchemilla vulgaris*

Found in moist pastures and the neighbourhood of streams, especially in hilly localities, although rather scarce in south-eastern England.

It is a perennial, and has a short, thick root-stock from which handsome leaves spread on very long footstalks. The leaves are roundish or kidney-shaped, cut into seven or nine lobes, with toothed edges. Each lobe is folded along the middle, and this pleating, combined with the pinked edge, suggested the name of Lady's Mantle.

The slender stem, a foot or eighteen inches long, is at first decumbent, afterwards assuming a more upright direction. The stem leaves are small and stalkless. The upper part of the stem branches into clustered sprays of tiny, yellow-green flowers, which have no petals. The pitcher-shaped calyx has five lobes and as many little bracts. Usually there are four perfect stamens attached to the mouth of the calyx. Nectar is secreted by a fleshy ring in the calyx-tube.

Flowering from June to August.

SALAD BURNET

Family ROSACEAE   *Poterium sanguisorba*

May be found abundantly
in dry pastures, especi-
ally in a chalky district.

It is a perennial. From
its stout rootstock springs
a rosette of radical leaves,
with ascending or erect
annual stems. The leaves
are all pinnate ; the
coarsely-toothed leaflets
in pairs, with a terminal
leaflet. The stems are
slender, branched, and
the flowers are gathered
into a purplish head.
They have no petals,
and are of two kinds ; the upper ones have a four-
lobed calyx with a narrow mouth, from which two
styles with brush-like stigmas are projected ; the
lower bear both stamens and stigmas, or stamens
only.

The stamens vary in number from twenty to
thirty, attached to the mouth of the calyx, and the
anthers hang out.

The leaves were formerly much used in the
salad-bowl, having a flavour very similar to that
of cucumber.

The flowering period is from June to August.

DOG ROSE

Family ROSACEAE   *Rosa canina*

In hedges and copses throughout Britain the Dog Rose may be found. It is the largest of the British wild roses.

The rootstock is woody, frequently producing suckers, from which rise the long, arching branches, covered with broad and sharp hooks, often reaching a length of six or eight feet, and forming a bush of considerable size.

The leaves are broken up into five or seven sharply-toothed leaflets.

The sweet-scented pink or white flowers are borne solitary or three or four together, at the ends of the branches, the large stipules of the undeveloped leaves forming elliptical bracts. The sepals are five in number, pinnate, and turned towards the stem, when the flower is open. There are five notched petals and many stamens. The styles are free and hairy. The ovary is sunk in the calyx, which changes to the pitcher-shaped scarlet fruits, known as " hips," in which are the hairy achenes.

The flowering period extends from June to August.

CRAB APPLE

Family ROSACEAE   *Malus sylvestris*

In woods and hedge-rows the Crab Apple may be found, as a rule, as a low tree, twenty or thirty feet high, sometimes more.

The branches frequently develop thorns, which indicate relationship with the wild plums.

Its leaves are of the rounded oblong shape, an inch or two long, toothed, and on long stalks.

The flowers are borne in few-flowered umbels, and the rosy undersides of the five petals give the tree a beauty that no other species of this group possesses.

These flowers are an inch or more across, of the usual rose type ; the five separate carpels are ultimately buried in the fleshy upgrowth of the flower-stalk, and become the " core " of the golden-yellow or fiery-red globular fruit, an inch or so in diameter. Their stigmas mature before the anthers, so that, as their abundant supplies of nectar induces many insects to visit them, there is sufficient provision made for cross-fertilization.

The flowers usually appear in May.

AGRIMONY

Family ROSACEAE   *Agrimonia eupatoria*

Growing frequently by the roadside, borders of fields and waste places, this is one of the prettiest of our wayside plants.

It is perennial. From the short and woody rootstock rise the erect, hairy stems, two or three feet high.

The leaves are " interruptedly " pinnate, more or or less clothed with soft hairs, the leaflets increasing in size as they near the terminal leaflet.

The golden - starred flowers are borne on the long, leafless flower-stalk in the form of a raceme, in which each flower is attached to the central stem by a stalk of its own.

The flowers consist of a top-shaped tubular and spiny calyx, with contracted mouth and five overlapping lobes ; five golden petals, ten or more stamens, and two carpels sunk in the calyx-tube, their styles and two-lobed stigmas protruding.

As the lower fruits ripen the raceme lengthens, and the calyx-tubes and their spines harden and assume a drooping position, owing to the downward curving of their little footstalks.

Flowering all the summer.

ENCHANTER'S NIGHTSHADE

Family ONAGRACEAE   *Circaea lutetiana*

Along the glades of damp woods, beside the thickets and undergrowths, will be found this tall, slender plant.

The rounded stem, with its long-stalked, large, oval, opposite leaves, terminates in a long, branched raceme of pale pink flowers. The margins of the leaves are faintly toothed. If the downy leaves are held to the light the leaf-stalk will be seen to be studded with pellucid dots. Some of the lower leaves are as much as three inches long.

The pink flowers are only about one-eighth of an inch across, and are remarkable for all their parts being in twos. The hairy, tubular calyx has two lobes, there are two heart-shaped petals, two pink stamens, and the ovary is two-celled, and when it develops into an egg-shaped fruit, covered with hooked bristles, it will be found to contain two seeds.

The flowering period extends from June to late in August.

ROSE-BAY WILLOW-HERB

Family ONAGRACEAE *Chamaenerion angustifolium*

On moist banks, moist open woods, chiefly on light soils, this handsome plant may be found.

It has a perennial, creeping rootstock, from which rise the annual, erect stems, smooth and unbranched, from two to four feet high.

The leaves are lance-shaped, stalked and alternate.

The large rosy-purple flowers, about one inch across, form an elegant raceme. There are four purple sepals and four petals which are not opposite, but paired irregularly. There are eight down-bent stamens, of which four are long, and four short. When the flower opens the anthers shed their pollen, but until all the pollen has been shed, the short style is curved downwards ; then it quickly elongates, and its clubbed head separates into four stigmas. After fertilization, what appeared to be the long stalk of the flower enlarges until it is stout, square and three or four inches long. This is really the stalked ovary, which in due time splits open and reveals the egg-shaped seeds.

Flowering from July to August.

PURPLE LOOSESTRIFE

Family LYTHRACEAE　　　　　*Lythrum salicaria*

The Purple Loosestrife may be found in marshy places and on the banks of streams.

It has a perennial creeping rootstock, from which rise the annual, angled stems, attaining a height from three to five feet, branched and bearing opposite, or whorled, entire lance-shaped leaves which clasp the stem at the base.

The starry flowers are bright reddish-purple, about an inch in diameter, forming a dense terminal spike, consisting of a cylindrical calyx - tube with twelve teeth, of which the alternate ones are awl-shaped and longer than the others; four to six oblong petals, a two-celled ovary and twelve stamens.

The flowers are produced in three forms on different individuals, and known as *trimorphic*. There is a long-styled, a short-styled and a mid-styled form, and each of these forms possesses two sets of stamens, and pollen grains that vary in size, in proportion to the length of the stamens.

Flowering from July to September.

WHITE BRYONY

Family CUCURBITACEAE   *Bryonia dioica*

Common in woods and thickets in the south of England, but rare in the north.

It is a perennial with a thick rootstock, from which rise several shoots covered with bristles, which grow into long, trailing stems with a number of tendrils that coil spirally.

The stalked leaves are four or five inches across, heart-shaped, and cut up into from three to seven lobes, each deeply toothed.

The flowers are of two kinds, borne by the same plant; with stamens only, or with ovary and stigmas only; sometimes on separate plants. The calyx and corolla are the same in both, but the female flowers are known by the globular ovary beneath the calyx. The calyx-tube is bell-shaped, with five teeth, and the corolla is cut into five segments of a greenish-white tint. The stamens are three, occasionally five. The style is divided into three stigmas. The pistillate flowers develop into red berries, when ripe, and contain three to six seeds.

Flowering from May to September.

WALL PENNYWORT

Family CRASSULACEAE *Umbilicus rupestris*

Known also as Navelwort and Penny - pies. It should be looked for in crevices of rocks and on stone-built hedges along the western coasts of England and Scotland and in Ireland. It extends more sparingly along the south coast as far as Kent.

It is a perennial with a tuberous rootstock, from which springs a loose cluster of thick, circular leaves on long stalks. The footstalk is attached to the centre of the leaf, whose upper surface has a deep depression at that point, and is two or three inches across, with notched margins.

From these radical leaves rises the flowering stem, which bears leaves of a different shape; the lower ones spoon-shaped, the upper wedge-shaped.

The flower stem may rise to a height of three feet, closely set all round with drooping greenish-white flowers. They consist of five sepals, a long tubular corolla with the mouth four- or five-lobed; ten stamens and five pistils with thread-like styles.

Flowering from May to August.

WILD CELERY

Family UMBELLIFERAE   *Apium graveolens*

This is really the plant from which the crisp, sweet stalks of our table celery have been evolved by the gardener, though in its wild state it is acrid, coarse and probably poisonous.

It grows in ditches and marshy places not far from the sea.

It is a perennial with a tap-root and a stout furrowed stem about two feet in height.

The large smooth leaves are either pinnate or divided into three wedge-shaped leaflets, which are cut and lobed, and the lower ones stalked.

The numerous greenish-white flowers are borne on short pedicels, in compound umbels, and the petal tips are greatly curved inwards. There are no bracts.

The very small fruit is roundish, laterally compressed ; carpels five angled, with a solitary vitta alternating with the primary ridges.

The flowering period extends from June to August.

FOOL'S PARSLEY

Family UMBELLIFERAE   *Aethusa cynapium*

A common weed in fields and gardens, abundant in England and extending to southern Scotland.

It is an annual. Its rootstock is spindle-shaped and fleshy, and the round, hollow stem, rising to one or two feet high, is branched and marked with fine longitudinal lines.

The smooth, compound leaves are bluish-green in tint. The wedge-shaped leaflets are themselves pinnate, and the pinnæ are lobed.

The white flowers are small and irregular, and are grouped in small umbels, which are again gathered into large umbels of umbels. The small umbels are provided with an involucre, consisting of three or five bracteoles, very slender and hanging downward; but the compound umbel has no bract. This feature is a peculiar character of the species.

The entire plant is evil-smelling and said to be poisonous.

Flowering during July and August.

WATER DROPWORT

Family UMBELLIFERAE   *Oenanthe fistulosa*

May be found in most ditches, rivulets and marshes throughout England, Ireland and southern Scotland.

It is a perennial with fleshy, fibrous roots that burrow deeply into the mud, and are often swollen and tuberous. The erect rounded stems, rising to a height of two or three feet, are slightly branched.

The leaves are pinnate ; those from the root with small wedge-shaped segments, those from the stem with the segments fewer and narrower.

The umbel terminating the stem consists of three partial-umbels of tiny white flowers, all of which are fertile ; but the branches bear umbels with a great number of parts and sterile flowers.

The individual fruits are about a quarter of an inch long, angular, with the two spiny styles still attached.

The flowering period extends from July to September.

ANGELICA

Family UMBELLIFERAE   *Angelica sylvestris*

This handsome plant may be found in copses, on the margin of damp woods, and in the neighbourhood of streams throughout the country.

It is a perennial, and its stout, hollow stem may attain a height of anything from five to nine feet; it is tinged with purple, with fine grooves and ridges.

The triangular leaves, two or three feet long, have stout stalks, which expand greatly where they embrace the stem. The leaves are broken up into several paired divisions, and these are divided again into three pairs and an odd one of lance-shaped leaflets.

Above the leaves the stem branches, each ending in a large compound umbel of white or pale purple flowers. The petals are nearly equal, giving a regularity to the flower; soon after opening the long stamens are more conspicuous than the petals.

The fruit consists of two compressed oval carpels, whose outer ridges are expanded to form wings.

Flowering from July to September.

HOG-WEED

Family UMBELLIFERAE *Heracleum sphondylium*

In moist hedgerow and waste almost everywhere, the Hog-weed or Cow Parsnip is to be found.

It is a conspicuous and coarse-growing plant, and has a thick, grooved and hairy stem, which commonly attains a height of from four to six feet. It is hollow, and its upper portion is branched.

The broad, lower leaves, frequently as much as three feet in length, are pinnate in form, with the leaflets lobed and toothed. The upper leaves are similar, but smaller.

The flower head consists of a large umbel, of about twenty rays, forming a massive head of flowers, varying from white to pink ; the outer ring of flowers much larger and very irregular in form.

The two carpels develop into slightly convex, shield-shaped fruits, suspended from the upper part of their inner surface by attachment to the tip of a bristle. Within each of the fruits there is a single flat seed.

Flowering from June to September.

BEAKED PARSLEY

Family UMBELLIFERAE   *Anthriscus sylvestris*

Nearly every ditch and hedgebank in the country is beautified by the presence of the Beaked Parsley or Wild Chervil, with its delicate umbel of flowers, and its profusion of leaves of lace-like fineness.

It is a biennial and its stock descends into a taproot. The stem is stout and hollow, and attains a height of three or four feet, hairy below, smooth above, and furrowed throughout. The fernlike leaves are downy, wedge-shaped, twice or thrice pinnate, the leaflets again cut pinnately, and toothed.

The stem terminates in a light cluster of umbels, which has no bracts at its base, though the simple umbels have lance-shaped bracteoles, which are green, more or less tinged with pink, and either turned down or spread out.

The small flowers are white, and the point of each petal is turned over towards the centre of the flower.

The fruits are about a third of an inch in length, smooth and without ribs or vittæ.

Flowering in May and June.

EARTH-NUT

Family UMBELLIFERAE   *Conopodium majus*

Known also as Pig-nut, it is to be found in woods, heaths and pastures, but is by no means conspicuous, as it grows low amidst the herbage.

It is perennial and has a tuberous root-stock, growing as large as a chestnut and brown in colour. It may be eaten raw, but it is said to be best when boiled, or roasted like a chestnut, which it much resembles.

It has a tough, slender stem, with few leaves. The leaf is divided into three parts, and each of these is cut up into thread-like portions, but the general outline is broad wedge-shape, on a slender footstalk.

The small white flowers terminate the stem in the form of a compound umbel. There are no bracts, either to the partial or compound umbels. The petals are heart-shaped with a turned-in point.

When first the umbels open they assume a nodding attitude, but afterwards become erect.

Flowering throughout the summer.

HEDGE PARSLEY

Family UMBELLIFERAE   *Torilis japonica*

On hedgebanks and waste places throughout the country the Hedge Parsley may be found, after the Beaked Parsley has ceased blooming. For this reason, though equally common, it is not nearly so well known.

It is an annual. The erect stem, from two to three feet high, is solid, finely grooved, and covered with hairs that turn downwards. The hairy lower leaves are broken up into several lance-shaped leaflets, which are cut into lobes and large teeth ; the upper leaves, at the base of the branches, are simpler, slender and deeply toothed.

The stem is branched, each branch terminated by a compound umbel of minute white or pink flowers, with four or six awl-shaped bracts beneath it. The petals are more or less equal in size.

The fruits are oval and covered with awl-shaped spines.

The flowering period is from July to September

WILD CARROT

Family UMBELLIFERAE   *Daucus carota*

In hedges, waste corners of fields and by the roadsides, the Wild Carrot is conspicuous.

It is an annual or biennial. It has a dry stick-like tap-root from which rises the solid, tough, branched stem, which is ridged and grooved and densely clothed with white hairs.

The leaves are pinnate, like ferns, and the undersides are hairy.

The small white flowers are arranged in umbels, and some forty or fifty umbels are gathered together in a saucer-shaped head.

Each petal is notched on its outer edge, and a portion turned over towards the ovary. The little bracts of the small umbels are simple and lance-shaped. The bracts of the compound umbel are much broader, and deeply cut into about seven narrow segments.

The fruits are oblong and convex, each carpel with seven ridges, four of which are armed with long, curved spines, and pierced with oil-tubes (*vittæ*).

Flowering from May to August.

HEMLOCK

Family UMBELLIFERAE   *Conium maculatum*

Generally distributed, it
will be found growing
in all sorts of waste
places, along hedges and
banks of streams.

It has a biennial or
perennial tap-root, from
which rises a smooth
stem, more or less
spotted with dull purple
and attaining a height
of two to six feet, with
many branches from
the upper part.

The fern-like leaves
are alternate, large,
wedge-shaped and com-
pound, the leaflets
opposite, distant, and
deeply cut in a pinnate
manner.

The small white flowers are in small umbels,
and about a dozen of these are gathered into one
large terminal compound umbel. At the base of
each little umbel there are three short bracts, all
turned to one side (*unilateral*). The involucre
of the general flower cluster is composed of a
large number of bracts. The tips of the petals
are turned inwards.

The fruits are in pairs, their inner faces flat,
with thick, prominent wavy ridges.

Flowering in June and July.

MISTLETOE

Family LORANTHACEAE   *Viscum album*

It is found chiefly in the south and west of England, and is most likely to be seen growing upon Poplar and Apple.

It is an evergreen semi-parasite shrub. The seed germinates in a crevice of the bark of the host tree and the root takes the form of suckers, which penetrate the wood and branches among the tissues.

The short stem and its branches are round, and clothed with a smooth, yellow-green bark ; the branches fork repeatedly, and bear at their ends two, sometimes three, leathery leaves.

The small, yellowish flowers appear at the forking of the branches. The male flowers, usually in clusters of three ; the females may be in fives. In the females, the one-celled ovary is below the calyx, and has a simple stigma without a style. This develops into a pearly-white berry containing a single seed, which takes more than a year to ripen. It is indebted to birds for the distribution of its seeds.

Flowering from March to May.

MOSCHATEL

Family ADOXACEAE   *Adoxa moschatellina*

In woods and moist shady places the Moschatel is somewhat local but very abundant where it occurs.

It is perennial. From a tuberous root run creeping rootstocks, from which rise the erect, square stems, about four inches high, each bearing a pair of leaves. Each stem-leaf is cut into three leaflets; but those which spring direct from the rootstock may be cut into either one or two sets of three leaflets, usually three-lobed.

At the summit of the stem, there is a yellow-green flower, whose parts are in fours, whilst immediately below it are four others, with the parts, usually in fives.

The two- or three-lobed calyx forms a broad, open cup. The corolla is known as *rotate*, in which the lobes appear to be rotating. The stamens are in pairs, and the attachment of the anthers to the corolla tube is known as *peltate*. The short style separates into three or five stigmas, and the ovary develops into a green berry.

Flowering from March to May.

IVY

Family ARALIACEAE   *Hedera helix*

Common everywhere. In old woods and against ancient walls, it may almost be considered as a tree, for though it does not stand alone, its trunk may be found nearly a foot in diameter.

It is an evergreen, perennial climber. Its leaves are subject to great variation in form, though one dominant character runs through them all, except its upper leaves, which are totally unlike. Its five-lobed leaves are for its trailing and climbing branches, but when it reaches the top of wall or tree they become simple lance-shaped, and in the autumn these branches are crowned with its umbels of yellow-green flowers.

The flower consists of a calyx with five teeth, petals and stamens five each, style one with five obscure stigmas. The flowers are succeeded by blackish berries, sometimes yellow.

There is a common woodland variety, with smaller, narrower leaves, that never flowers ; neither do those forms that persistently trail along the hedge-bottom instead of climbing.

Flowering in September and October.

HONEYSUCKLE

Family CAPRIFOLIACEAE   *Lonicera periclymenum*

Widely distributed in hedges, copses and on heaths, this is one of the most familiar of our wild flowers. It owes its popularity not only to the beauty of its flowers, but also to its sweet scent and twining habit.

The stem is tough, attaining a length of from ten to twenty feet, and always twines from left to right. The leaves are egg-shaped and attached in pairs, the lower ones by short stalks, the upper ones stalkless.

The yellow flowers, tinged with red, are clustered, the five-toothed calyces closely crowded ; the corolla-tube, one or two inches long and divided into five lobes, which split irregularly into two opposite lips. It is rich in nectar, the corolla being often half-filled with it, and consequently it is a great favourite with insects, who are bound to take pollen from the outstanding anthers of one plant and deposit it upon the stigma of another.

The flowers are succeeded by a cluster of round crimson berries.

Flowering summer and autumn.

GOOSE-GRASS

Family RUBIACEAE   *Galium aparine*

To be found in hedges and thickets throughout Britain, where it forms dense hanging masses, often like curtains, the whole plant being covered with flinty hooks. It is also known as Cleavers.

It is an annual, and its stems extend to several feet, scrambling over bushes, to which it clings. The leaves are borne in whorls of from four to ten, at distant intervals on the square stem. They vary from six to eight, the flower-cymes springing from their axils.

The minute greenish-white flowers have three or four leaves at the base of the cyme, the calyx a mere ring, and the honeyed corolla, four or five lobed. There are four stamens, and two styles, united at their bases.

The fruits are green at first, then becoming purplish. These fruits are double and bristling with hooked spines, that cling to fur or feather, and are by this method distributed throughout the length and breadth of these islands.

Flowering in June and July.

HEDGE BEDSTRAW

Family RUBIACEAE   *Galium mollugo*

A favourite position for the Hedge Bedstraw is the upper part of a grassy hedgebank, but from its size and habitat, it is liable to be mistaken for Goose-grass, although a slight examination will show its distinctness.

It is a perennial and has long, weak stems, three to five feet long, not so stiff and brittle as those of the Goose-grass, smooth or hairy, and *without* hooks. The angles of the stem rough or hairy.

The leaves are broader than those of the Goose-grass and variable in form and size, with bristles on their margins, and generally six or eight in a whorl.

The small, white flowers are borne in large, panicled, horizontal cymes, rising from the axils of the leaves.

The fruits are much smaller than those of Goose-grass, and are black and rough, but without the hooked bristles.

The flowering period extends from June to August.

SPUR VALERIAN

Family VALARIANACEAE *Centranthus ruber*

The noblest of our wall-plants. It may be found on old walls, and occasionally in chalk-pits and railway cuttings. It is not truly wild in this country, but a visitor from the Continent that has become naturalized.

It is perennial, and has a branched, woody stock, from which rise many tough, round branches. The thick, stalkless, grey-green leaves are lance-shaped, their broad bases, sometimes, with a few coarse teeth. The crimson flower-head is bluntly conical. The calyx is a thickened margin to the ovary, which, after the fall of the corolla, unrolls and develops into a feathery *pappus*. The five-lobed corolla is long and tubular, ending in a hollow spur, which contains nectar. Sometimes the corolla is white. The pistil, with a slightly enlarged stigma, extends slightly beyond the corolla. The stamen is solitary, with a purplish anther. There is a faint sweet perfume from the flowers, and the root is also scented.

The flowering period extends from **May to September.**

WILD TEASEL

Family DIPSACACEAE　　　　　　*Dipsacus fullonum*

To be found in copse or hedgerow, roadsides and waste places, especially in the southern and midland counties of England.

It is a biennial, and during the first year has only radical leaves, that lie flat on the ground about eighteen inches across, in the form of a rosette. The second season it sends up stout, angular and spiny stems, about five or six feet high, crowned by the prickly cylindrical heads of purplish flowers. The stem-leaves are opposite, the lower couples joined together by their bases, forming a large cup, in which rain and dew collect and drowning many insects, their dissolved remains being absorbed by the plant for its partial sustenance.

The flower-head has an involucre of from eight to twelve slender, spiny bracts, curving upwards. The corolla has four short lobes, tubular and unequal.

Flowering in August and September.

LADY'S BEDSTRAW

Family RUBIACEAE   *Galium verum*

On dry banks and downs, the conspicuous colonies of the Lady's Bedstraw, may be found abundant throughout Britain.

It is a perennial. The woody, creeping rootstock forms runners from which rise the more or less erect, smooth and square stems, much branched at the base, from six inches to a foot long. The very slender leaves have their margins turned down, and their tips ending in a hard point. They are in whorls of from eight to twelve.

The very numerous small, yellow flowers are borne in dense cymes which, in the mass, make the plant a very conspicuous feature. The fruits are small and smooth.

One of its local names is Cheese-rennet, from a former use of the flowers to curdle milk for making cheese. It has also been used as a dye, and it is said that when animals feed upon it it reddens their bones.

The flowering period extends from June to September.

WOODRUFF

Family RUBIACEAE   *Galium odoratum*

In woods and shady places, especially amongst the leaf-mould of beech woods, the close patches of Woodruff may be found. A good old-fashioned favourite, better known to our grandmothers than to the present generation for giving a pleasant odour to the clean linen folded away in the linen press, as it is when its juices are drying up, after the plant is gathered, that it yields the sweet scent of new-mown hay. When growing it is only slightly odoriferous.

It is a perennial with a thin rootstock that creeps underground. Its slender erect stems attain a height of about a foot. The neat, smooth leaves are borne in whorls of seven, eight or nine leaves.

The minute, ivory-white funnel-shaped flowers terminate the stems, and are borne in a loose cyme, and are succeeded by tiny fruits that are covered with barbed bristles.

The flowering period is during May and June.

FIELD SCABIOUS

Family DIPSACACEAE   *Knautia arvensis*

In dry fields and on downs, and cultivated places throughout Britain, the Field Scabious may be found.

It is a perennial. Its hairy stem rises from a stout rootstock to the height of from one to three feet. The leaves vary considerably in different specimens, but usually those from the root are entire, of an oblong lance-shape, with toothed margins. The radical leaves are usually stalked.

The flower - heads are borne on a long, stout stalk and consist of about fifty florets, increasing in size from the centre to the outer margin, and of a pale blue or lilac colour, the central ones more inclined to red. The anthers are yellow. The corollas are usually four-lobed, those of the outer florets forming two lips.

The involucral bracts are broad and leaf-like, in two rows.

The flowering period is from June to September.

GOLDEN ROD

Family COMPOSITAE   *Solidago virgaurea*

Found throughout the country in oakwoods, heathlands, stony banks and rocky hillsides on a sandy soil.

It is a perennial, with an erect, slightly angular, smooth or downy stem, attaining a height of from one to three feet, except when growing up sea-cliffs, when it may be reduced to a few inches. The leaves are lance-shaped, with slightly toothed edges, and arranged alternately on the stem ; the lower ones are stalked.

The upper half of the stem bears numerous short branches, each supporting three or four slender flower-heads, the whole of them constituting a long, golden-yellow spray.

The lower part of the head is covered by over-lapping bracts, with thin margins, and the ray-florets are few. The darker disk-florets only slightly exceed them in number.

The downy fruit has a white pappus.

There is another species (*S. cambrica*) that occurs on mountains, which has a stem only a few inches high, with broader leaves and with fewer and larger flower-heads.

Flowering from July to September.

HEMP AGRIMONY

Family COMPOSITAE   *Eupatorium cannabinum*

It is abundant where the soil is damp, especially in the south of England; somewhat rare in Scotland. In woods or on the banks of rivers, when growing apart from undergrowth, where it has room to show itself, it is a fine plant.

It is a perennial, with a woody rootstock, from which rise its rounded, downy stems up to three or four feet high, and which are branched at the top.

The leaves are opposite, and broken up into three or five lance-shaped, saw-toothed leaflets, which are from two to four inches long.

Terminating the stem are the flower-heads, gathered into dense corymbs on the flowering branches. The involucral bracts are narrow, dry and translucent.

It is the simplest of our composite flowers, each flower-head consisting of very few flowers, which are tubular, and with five or six florets only, which have the mouth of the tube cleft into five lobes, and contain five anthers and a long, branched style.

Flowering from July to October.

DAISY

Family Compositae

Bellis perennis

This commonest of wild flowers may be found everywhere.

It is perennial and has a fleshy rootstock, several inches in length, from which the spoon-shaped leaves are produced in a rosette. The flower stem rises from the centre to a height of two to five inches.

The flower-head is composed of a conical receptacle, forming a small platform, on which are crowded together about 250 small flowers (*florets*). They take two forms—the central yellow or *disk-florets* are tubular, whilst those outside them are white and flat (*ray-florets*).

Each disk-floret has five lobes, and the tubular corolla has been formed by the union of five petals. The anthers are also united at their edges, containing the style, with the two branches of its stigma pressed tightly together.

The ray-florets invariably close up over the disk-florets at night and in wet weather, thereby fertilizing the stigmas by being brought into contact with the pollen of the disk-florets.

Flowering practically all the year round.

SEA ASTER

Family COMPOSITAE   *Aster tripolium*

To be found upon salt-marshes along any of our coasts, extending to the north of Scotland. Known also as Starwort.

It is a perennial. From spindle-shaped root rises a stout, erect stem, slightly branched, two or three feet high. The long, smooth, fleshy leaves are lance-shaped, sometimes slightly toothed. Each branch ends in a cluster of fragrant purple-violet flowers of the Daisy type of structure, a composite head of tubular, yellow disk-florets, surrounded by a single whorl of ray-florets which vary in colour to almost white. The disk-florets contain both stamens and pistil, but the ray-florets are female only. Each head is about two-thirds of an inch across.

The flowering period is from July to September.

OX-EYE DAISY

Family COMPOSITAE

Chrysanthemum leucanthemum

It is abundant, often too much so, in hayfields, pastures and on banks, etc., throughout Britain. Known also as Dog Daisy, and in Scotland, where the Daisy is called a Gowan, it is known by the name of Horse-Gowan.

It is a perennial, with slightly branched, erect stems, rising to a height of one or two feet.

The radical leaves, on long stalks, are coarsely toothed. The stem leaves are narrow, deeply toothed and without stalks.

The solitary flower-head, on long stems, consists of an involucre of three or four series of scales with thin, brown, or purple edges, overlapping each other after the manner of the tiles on a roof. In other respects it resembles the Daisy. The ray-florets are white and the disk-florets numerous and golden-yellow.

The flowering period extends from May to August.

COMMON FLEABANE

Family COMPOSITAE   *Pulicaria dysenterica*

A common plant in marshy places, on ditch-banks, and by the side of rivers. Abundant in the south of England, rarer in the north and very scarce in Scotland.

It is a perennial, with a creeping root-stock, from which rise erect, branching, downy stems to a height of about a foot. The leaves are much wrinkled and downy, of an oblong heart-shape with toothed edges, their base partially embracing the stem.

The bright yellow flower-head, which is really a vast assemblage of flowers, closely packed upon a common *receptacle*, is about one inch across, produced at the ends of the branches. The ray-florets are developed into long, slender straps (*ligules*), and contain no stamens. The involucre is woolly and its scales are bristly.

Formerly it was used as a medicine, in cases of dysentery.

The flowering period extends from July to September.

SCENTLESS MAYWEED

Family COMPOSITAE *Tripleurospermum maritimum*

In fields, hedges and on waste places throughout Britain the Scentless Mayweed may be found. Known also as the Corn Mayweed. So closely does this plant resemble the Corn Chamomile that, at a little distance, they appear alike, but a touch will prove which is which. Whilst the Chamomile exhales the sweet perfume identified with its name, the Mayweed is scentless.

It is an annual or biennial, with erect, branching stems, well clothed with alternate, stalkless leaves. These look as though designed for a submerged aquatic plant, they are so finely cut up into many exceedingly slender segments. If closely examined it will be seen that there is a very distinct *pinnate* arrangement, and that the segments are themselves pinnate.

The large flower-head, about two inches across, is supported by a long, smooth stalk ; the white ray-florets large and ultimately drooping, and the yellow disk convex. The involucral bracts are edged with brown. There is no perceptible odour.

The flowering period is from June to October.

CORN CHAMOMILE

Family COMPOSITAE *Anthemis arvensis*

The Corn Chamomile will be found exceedingly common in the fields and waste places of some localities, whilst in other districts it is rare. Though somewhat widely distributed it is a local plant.

It is an annual. The lower portion of its stem is prostrate, sending up erect branches, with alternate, prettily cut leaves, twice pinnate.

The flower - heads are borne singly on long stalks, and the floral envelope (*involucre*) consists of a number of overlapping scales (*bracts*), whose margins are dry and chaffy. The base (*receptacle*) upon which the florets are packed is convex and covered with little chaffy scales which stand up between the florets. The yellow disk-florets contain both anthers and pistil ; the white ray-florets are pistillate only.

The whole plant is downy with minute silky hairs.

The flowering period extends from May to August.

YARROW

Family COMPOSITAE *Achillea millefolium*

One of our commonest weeds in pastures, on commons and roadside wastes. It is known also as Milfoil.

It has a perennial, creeping rootstock from which the radical leaves spring directly. The erect flowering-stem attains a height of about a foot. Its leaves are cut up into a large number of segments, very slender and crowded, and are again cut up ; so that the general aspect of the leaf is exceedingly light and feathery. Those given off by the flowering-stem become more simple as they near the summit.

Unlike as the flowers may at first sight appear to those of the Daisy and Dandelion, those of the Yarrow are of the same order. The white or pinkish ray-florets, of which there are only five or six, are pistillate only, but the yellow disk-florets are tubular and contain both anthers and stigmas. The large number of flower-heads are arranged to form a corymb.

Flowering from June to the end of the year.

TANSY

Family COMPOSITAE  *Chrysanthemum vulgare*

Growing in waste places by field and roadside throughout the country, the Tansy is believed to be a garden escape, or its descendant, that has become naturalized. Certainly there was a time when every kitchen garden had its clump of Tansy, for it was a valued item in cookery, especially in the spring-time.

It is a perennial, with a creeping rootstock, from which rise beautiful broad, feathery, radical leaves, and flowering stems reaching a height of two or three feet.

The leaves are very deeply divided in a pinnate or bi-pinnate manner, the segments toothed. The angled stem branches off into a corymb of flower-heads. Each flower-head is enclosed in a half-rounded involucre of leathery bracts. There is an outer row of very short ray-florets, of the same golden-yellow colour as the disk-florets; they are pistillate only, whilst the disk-florets are all staminate.

Flowering from July to September.

MUGWORT

Family COMPOSITAE   *Artemisia vulgaris*

By the roadsides and waste places throughout the country the Mugwort may be found.

It is a perennial, aromatic herb, much used in earlier days to impart a bitter flavour to drink.

From its thick and woody rootstock rises the red, rough stem from two to four feet high, shrubby at the base and branched above.

The leaves are alternate, much cut into sharp-pointed segments, and silvery - white beneath with silky down. They are arranged alternately on the stems ; they are stalked and the margins of the segments are turned back.

The flower-heads are small and are gathered into many short, woolly spikes. They contain but a few tubular reddish-yellow flowers. The outer flowers contain no stamens, and the corolla has but three teeth. The inner ones have five teeth and contain only stamens, or stamens and pistil.

Flowering from June to September.

COLTSFOOT

Family COMPOSITAE 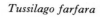 *Tussilago farfara*

The Coltsfoot may be found in waste cultivated places, especially where the soil is stiff and clayey.

Its thick, perennial rootstock has many burrowing offshoots, from which rise direct the large, cobwebby leaves, of a broad heart-shape, that may become nearly a foot across, the edges angled and toothed, and the undersides white with cottony down.

The flower-stem is a tall, hollow scape that is covered with long, woolly scales, which supports the solitary bright yellow flower. The slender ray-florets of the flower are female, and the style pushes up through the tube of stamens, and the two stigmatic arms are united.

The flower passes, the scape lengthens and supports a hoary head of soft *pappus*, or down, to which the fruits are attached.

The Coltsfoot used to have a very popular reputation as a curer of coughs and healer of chest complaints, and it is still used in a small way for that purpose.

The flowers usually appear some time in March.

BUTTERBUR

Family COMPOSITAE

Petasites hybridus

Frequently to be found in meadows, on banks of streams or roadsides where the soil is sandy.

It is a perennial, and its flowers appear before the leaves, which are, roughly speaking, kidney-shaped with irregular teeth, and often as much as three feet in diameter. They are white underneath and cobwebby both above and below in their young state, but the upper surface afterwards becomes clean. They have long, thick leaf-stalks.

In the pinkish flower-heads there are male heads and female heads, though each head contains a few flowers of either sex. The two forms are produced by separate plants. The male floret is bell-shaped, the mouth cut into five lobes ; the female is a slender tube with a protruding pistil. All the flower-heads are gathered into a large dense panicle, contained in two very large bracts. The upper heads open first.

It is a boon to bee-keepers, for its numerous flowers are rich in nectar.

Flowering from March to May.

GROUNDSEL

Family COMPOSITAE   *Senecio vulgaris*

To be found almost everywhere in Britain, and one of those weeds that love to avail themselves of man's labour in loosening the soil for them ; but as there is nothing woody about it, it never becomes a real nuisance to the cultivator.

It is an annual, with an erect, branching stem about six inches high. The leaves are alternate, deeply cut and the lobes irregularly toothed.

The flower-heads form terminal corymbs and the involucres consist of about twenty bracts. The ray-florets are usually wanting, and consequently the few cylindrical flower-heads have a very singular appearance. The flowers are succeeded by the well-known fluffy pappus attached to the seeds It is this hoary head of seed-bearers that has enabled the plant to become one of the most widely distributed in all temperate and cold climates.

There are about five hundred known species, of which, however, only nine are native to Britain.

It may be found in flower all the year round.

LESSER BURDOCK

Family COMPOSITAE   *Arctium minus*

Common in all waste places, the Burdock is well-known to country youth for its hooked bracts, which make the fruit-head an admirable instrument of torture, or an ornament for decorating a person's clothes.

It is a biennial with a stout, branching stem reaching a height of three or four feet. Occasionally, in out-of-the-way corners, it may attain a height of six or seven feet.

The fine, bold lower leaves are heart-shaped and have a densely cottony underside, the upper leaves much smaller and alternate.

The flowers are in dense heads, like a thistle, but without any spreading rays. The involucre is globose, of many leathery bracts, each ending in a long stiff hook, by means of which the ripe heads become firmly attached to the fur of animals, and the seeds are thus carried far and wide. The purple corolla has five lobes.

Flowering from June to September.

RAGWORT

Family COMPOSITAE   *Senecio jacobaea*

By the roadsides, in waste places and on neglected land the Ragwort may be found almost everywhere.

It is a perennial, and has an erect, branching, leafy stem, from two to four feet high. The general form of the leaf is lyrate, but it is broken up by pinnate divisions into toothed lobes to an extent that justifies its popular name. The upper leaves have no stalks, and their connection with the stem is marked by a pair of auricles.

The bright yellow flower-heads are about one inch across, the rays spreading, and the involucre is bell-shaped. They form a compact, terminal corymb.

Known in Scotland as Stinking Willie on account of the unpleasant odour of the plant when bruised. To the agriculturist generally it is an absolute nuisance, though the ordinary rambler can afford to admire the sight of, sometimes, acres of land painted with its rich gold.

Flowering from June to October, but in the south it may be found in flower at Christmas.

SPEAR THISTLE

Family COMPOSITAE   *Cirsium vulgare*

This species will be found in almost any pasture, hedgeside or on waste ground.

It is sometimes annual, sometimes biennial, and is a sturdy giant of its race, the stout, erect, prickly stem being frequently five feet high. The lance-shaped leaves vary in length from six inches to a foot, and are deeply cut into strongly-toothed lobes, each lobe partly divided into two, and each division ending in a long, sharp spine. They are bristly above and cottony beneath.

The flower-heads terminate short branches, and are erect; the involucre is egg-shaped, cottony, and about one inch in diameter. Its very numerous bracts are narrow, ending in long, sharp spines.

From the narrow end of this egg-shaped mass the long, purple corolla-tubes break forth as a soft plume, to be succeeded by the silky down that buoys up the shining seeds in their autumnal dispersal far and wide.

Flowering from July to October.

SAW-WORT

Family COMPOSITAE   *Serratula tinctoria*

To be found among low bushes on the outskirts of woods, in copses and occasionally on heaths. Though common in England, it is entirely absent from some districts.

The slender, branching stem is two or three feet long, more or less erect and leafy. The leaves show considerable variation on the same plant; the lower ones being cut deeply into sharply-toothed, lance-shaped leaflets, the terminal one being the largest.

The flower-heads form a terminal corymb and are long, egg-shaped, covered with closely overlapping bracts, the inner ones being purplish. The florets are red-purple. An examination will reveal a difference between them: the male flowers have blue anthers, and the two arms of the style keep close together; the female have white anthers and the arms of the style spread widely apart. The male anthers are filled with pollen, the female anthers are not.

The rough, oblong fruits are covered by a tuft of pappus hairs.

Flowering from July to September.

MUSK THISTLE

Family COMPOSITAE   *Carduus nutans*

May be found on moorland wastes or in some sheltered hollow of the South Downs, where it is fairly frequent. The bold, dark leaves and large crimson flower-heads make the Musk Thistle a very handsome plant.

It is biennial. The stout, erect stem, without a branch, attains a height of from two to five feet, grooved, winged and spiny, a condition which is helped by the leaves extending partially down it, and investing it with their long spears.

The leaves are very pinnatified and very prickly, with interrupted wings.

The large, crimson flower-head, two inches or more across, hangs on its curved stalk in a drooping manner, giving out an agreeable scent, which has been compared to musk.

It is a fine object even before the flowers open, for the prickly bracts of the involucre are covered with a regular mesh of webbing, as though some industrious spider had been working upon it.

Flowering from June to the end of September.

HARD-HEADS

Family COMPOSITAE   *Centaurea scabiosa*

Known also as the Greater Knapweed, and closely allied to the thistles, in whose company it may be found, it must be sought for on dry wastes and in neglected corners of pastures.

It is a perennial, and its grooved, slightly branched stem rises to a height of two or three feet, covered with soft hairs.

The long leaves are much cut up into egg-shaped segments. Nearer the summit of the stem the leaves are simpler and reduced to a very slight width.

The globose flower-heads have for involucre a number of cottony scales, with dark brown margins and pale fringe. The ray-florets are bright purple, their free ends divided into five long, slender lobes. They are composite flowers, and they should afford interest to the rambler by instituting a comparison between them and the Daisies, or other of the composites.

The flowering period extends from July to September.

BRISTLY OX-TONGUE

Family COMPOSITAE   *Picris echioides*

Though quite a common plant in rough wastes, and by roadsides on stiff soils, it is frequently mistaken for the more familiar Sow - thistle. Like the Sow-thistles it is full of a bitter, milky juice.

It is annual or biennial, and its stout, branched stems rise to two or three feet high. The broad, lance-shaped root-leaves are stalked, but those on the stem are stalkless and heart-shaped.

The composite flower-head has five broad, heart-shaped involucral bracts which cover up the ordinary scales of the half-globular involucre. All the florets are strap-shaped, as in the Dandelion, and of a yellow hue. The stems and outer involucral bracts are marked with purplish-red. The flower-heads are succeeded by fluffy hemispheres of white pappus, as in the case of the Dandelion.

The whole plant is well covered with stiff hairs that branch into three minute hooks at their tips. These bristles spring from white, swollen bases.

Flowering from June to September.

GOAT'S-BEARD

Family COMPOSITAE   *Tragopogon pratensis*

Fairly common in meadows and wastes of England; much more rare in Scotland and Ireland.

It is biennial and has a tap-rootstock, similar to a parsnip, from which spring the long, curling, grass-like, stalkless leaves that clasp the stem by their bases. The erect, slightly branched stem attains a height of one or two feet.

The yellow flower-heads are solitary with eight involucral bracts united at the base. All the florets are rayed and contain both stamens and pistil. They are invested with pappus hairs which are stiff and feathered. It is from these *beards* the plant gets its English name.

One of the folk-names of this plant is " John-go-to-bed-at-noon," due to the fact that the flower is an inveterate early-closer, for it opens about four o'clock in the morning and closes by twelve, although flowers that have been fertilized early in the morning close much before that time.

Flowering in June and July.

WALL LETTUCE

Family COMPOSITAE   *Mycelis muralis*

Most frequent and most widely distributed of our native species, *M. muralis* cannot be described as an abundant weed. It is often found in the places suggested by its name, but also in the hedgerow and on rocky banks.

It is a smooth annual or biennial, with a tall, slender, branched stem, rising to a height of as much as three feet. The leaves are of the pattern known as *lyrate*, or lyre-shaped. The upper part is much lobed and jagged at the edges, whilst the lower portion is greatly attenuated. The upper leaves are narrow, clasping the stem, with prominent auricles.

The small, yellow flowers are composite, with strap-shaped outer rays, and are borne on slender pedicels.

The flowering period is from June to August.

LONG-ROOTED CAT'S-EAR

Family COMPOSITAE   *Hypochoeris radicata*

Plentiful in meadows, pastures and waste places throughout the country. In appearance it comes pretty close to the Hawkweeds, which roughly resemble it, especially in colour.

It is a perennial, with a tap-root, from which rises and spreads a circlet of many rough, hairy leaves, their edges scalloped ; there are no stem-leaves.

The flower-stem is branched, each branch bearing but one yellow flower-head, which is more than an inch across, and has a structure similar to that of the Dandelion and Chicory. The involucral bracts are in several series, laid one over the other like tiles. All the corollas are strap-shaped with five teeth at the free end.

The pappus or down that surrounds the fruit consists of a row of feathery hairs, surrounded by an outer row of shorter bristles. The flowers are longer than the involucre.

The flowering period extends from June to September.

DANDELION

Family COMPOSITAE   *Taraxacum officinale*

In meadows, pastures, cultivated and waste places everywhere the Dandelion is to be found.

It is a perennial. It has no proper stem, the leaves springing directly from the long, thick root, which is black on the outside and very bitter.

From their midst arise the golden-yellow flower-heads on their hollow stalks. Both stems and leaf-stalks exude a milky juice when broken. The involucre consists of a double row of bracts, the inner long and erect, the outer short, but turned back and clasping the stem.

The florets are all strap-shaped, and each is a perfect flower, containing both anther and stigma. The ovary is crowned by the corolla, which is invested by a pappus of soft, white, silky hairs, representing the calyx. After fertilization the corollas wither, the bracts open, and each pappus spreads into a parachute, the whole constituting a fluffy ball. A light wind detaches them and they float off to disperse the seeds far and wide.

Flowering from March to October.

CORN SOWTHISTLE

Family COMPOSITAE   *Sonchus arvensis*

May be found in or around cultivated fields and waste places, and is one of the most handsome of our native flowers.

It is a perennial, with a large, creeping rootstock, which sends off runners.

The hollow stem, rising to two or three feet high, sometimes reaches a height of five feet in moist ground. The stem is clasped by the bases of the finely-cut leaves. These are deeply lobed, and edged with sharp teeth ; the lower leaves have stalks, the upper have not.

The unopened involucre is very broad at the base, and covered all over—as are the stems also—with short hairs with glandular ends of a golden-yellow. The expanded bright golden-yellow flower-head is composed entirely of ray-florets and is about two inches across.

The flowering period is during August and September.

CHICORY

Family COMPOSITAE   *Cichorium intybus*

The Wild Chicory is peculiarly a plant of the dry roadside, especially in chalk districts, where it is a striking feature.

It is a perennial, with a long, thick, fleshy rootstock. Its radical leaves spread themselves out, rosette fashion, upon the ground; the few that are scattered alternately up the somewhat hairy stem, clasp the latter with the two lobes at their base. The tough, erect stem is grooved and the flowers are attached without the intervention of flower-stalks. The bright, pale-blue flowers are usually in pairs. The involucre consists of two series of bracts, the outer row being shorter than the inner, and turned back. There is no distinction between ray-florets and disk-florets; they are all strap-shaped and rather broad, with a straight end, notched into five teeth.

It is cultivated on a large scale on the Continent, for its root, when roasted and ground, forms the substance that is used in combination with coffee.

Flowering from July to October.

HAWKWEED

Family COMPOSITAE   *Hieraceum perpropinquum*

It will be found in copses and on hedge-banks from the south of England to the east of Scotland ; also in Ireland.

Like all the Hawk-weeds, it is a perennial with a tough stem from two to four feet high. Its radical leaves wither early, and the large number of stem-leaves, beginning some distance above the ground, are rather crowded, the upper ones progressively reduced in size ; the lower ones lance-shaped, with a few distant teeth whose points are directed forwards ; the small upper leaves are broader than long, with the base rounded or almost heart-shaped. The lower part of the stem is densely clothed with long, fine, white hairs.

The bright yellow flower-heads, which expand in succession, are about one inch across. The florets are strap-shaped with square ends, cut deeply into five teeth ; the long styles are dark-tinted. Later, pale-brownish pappus hairs crown a short, furrowed red fruit.

Flowering from July to September.

ROUND-HEADED RAMPION

Family CAMPANULACEAE *Phyteuma tenerum*

A ramble along the chalk-downs in Kent, Sussex, Surrey, or Wiltshire will almost certainly be rewarded by the discovery of the dark blue flowers of the Rampion, closely clustered in globose heads, swaying on their long stems.

It is a perennial of the Bellflower family, and has a tuberous rootstock, from which rise several more or less erect stems to a height of one or one and a half feet. The radical leaves (rarely visible when the the plant is in flower) have long stalks, and are oval lance-shaped, with rounded teeth on the margins. The few stem-leaves are stalkless, lance-shaped and progressively smaller.

Each stem ends in a solitary, dense head of dark-blue flowers, of which there may be forty in a single head. The corolla is cut into five slender lobes, which are at first united by their edges, but at length separate and spread widely.

Flowering in July and August.

NIPPLEWORT

Family COMPOSITAE   *Lapsana communis*

A common and widely distributed weed. It grows everywhere on waste ground and the borders of cultivated fields.

It is an annual. Its branched stem reaches a height of two or three feet, and its thin lower leaves are comparatively large, of a lyrate shape. There is a large terminal lobe, and a pair of narrow ones below it, the margins scalloped to produce distant teeth. The lance-shaped upper leaves are much smaller with their margins similarly toothed.

The flower-heads are small, containing few florets, which are all yellow and of the strap-shaped kind. The involucre consists of a single whorl of slender bracts. The bracts remain partially closed over the seeds (which have no pappus), the seed head retaining an oval shape, which appears to have suggested the popular name of the plant.

Dockorenes is another old English name for the plant, which was formerly used in salads.

Flowering from July to September.

SHEEP'S-BIT SCABIOUS

Family CAMPANULACEAE *Jasione montana*

The Sheep's-bit Scabious may be found on heath or down where the soil is light and dry.

It is annual or biennial. Several rough stems diverge from the rootstock and attain a height of about a foot. They have a few spreading branches, each branch ending in a hemispherical head of lilac-blue flowers about half an inch in diameter. There is a rosette of stalked, oblong leaves at the base, whilst those from the stem are much narrower and stalkless.

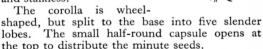

The corolla is wheel-shaped, but split to the base into five slender lobes. The small half-round capsule opens at the top to distribute the minute seeds.

This is the only British species.

The flowering period extends from June to September.

NETTLE-LEAVED BELLFLOWER

Family CAMPANULACEAE *Campanula trachelium*

This fine plant may be found in all its beauty in hillside woods and copses, and along the hedgerows, chiefly in the south.

It is a perennial with a stout, short rootstock, from which rise large, heart-shaped leaves on long stalks, coarsely toothed and bristly. The stem-leaves become less heart-shaped and more shortly stalked the farther they are from the roots ; but the aspect of the leafy stem before the flowers appear is very nettle-like. The angled and bristly stem attains a height of three or four feet, the upper half bearing many small racemes of more or less erect blue-purple bells, which are three-quarters of an inch across. The upper bud in each raceme opens first, the others in succession ; by this plan the entire panicle is kept well covered with open flowers until the end.

The Nettle-leaved Bellflower appears to be the original Canterbury Bell. Throatwort is another old English name for it.

Flowering from August to October.

HAREBELL

Family CAMPANULACEAE *Campanula rotundifolia*

On heaths, hilly pastures and roadsides the Harebell will be found abundant all over Britain.

It is a perennial with a slender, creeping rootstock, from which rise several very slender, often branched, angled stems six inches to a foot high. The first formed leaves, near the ground, are more or less heart-shaped and stalked, and usually die away at the time of flowering. The leaves that occur higher up the stem become more and more slender.

The delicately drooping blue flowers, swaying to the slightest breeze, consist of a beautiful bell-shaped corolla with five lobes, five stamens and a style with from three to five stigmas.

This is the true Bluebell of Scotland; the Bluebell of the southerner is the Wild Hyacinth.

The flowering period extends from July to September.

IVY-LEAVED BELLFLOWER

Family CAMPANULACEAE *Wahlenbergia hederacea*

By no means is this a common plant in this country. Its southern distribution is from Kent to Cornwall, and this is continued through the western counties as far north as Yorkshire. It is not confined altogether to bogland, but may sometimes be found among grass in the wetter parts of woods where there is peaty soil.

It is a perennial with a small, creeping rootstock, from which radiate trailing stems which are mere threads. The five-pointed, ivy-shaped leaves only slightly exceed half an inch at their fullest development. The long leaf-stalk is thicker at its junction with the leaf than at its lower extremity.

The flowers are solitary and borne erectly above the leaves on long foot-stalks, starting off from the stem opposite to a leaf. There is a top-shaped calyx with five triangular lobes, which clasp the base of the delicate pale-blue, bell-shaped corolla, which has five blunt-pointed lobes that turn slightly outwards.

Flowering during July and August.

VENUS'S LOOKING-GLASS

Family CAMPANULACEAE   *Legousia hybrida*

It may be looked for in corn-fields on dry soils, chiefly in the Eastern Counties, though its English distribution extends as far north as Durham.

Known also as Corn Bell-flower and Corn Violet.

It is an annual, from a few inches to a foot in height. The leaves are wavy-oblong, slightly toothed ; those from the roots with stalks, those from the stem without. The stem may be branched from the base, or entirely un-branched, angled and rough with minute hairs.

The flower—usually soli-tary at the end of the stem or branch—is singular in the length of the calyx tube, enclosing the ovary ; its lobes are somewhat leafy, longer than those of the corolla, which are lilac on the outside and blue within.

They are succeeded by angular capsules an inch or more long.

The flowering period extends from June to September.

Family ERICACEAE   *Erica tetralix*

May be found in damp hollows and boggy spots on the heath, and in the moister parts of pine-woods.

It is a shrub, one half to one and a half feet high. The stems are erect, branched and downy. The leaves are in whorls of four round the stem, their margins turned under. and fringed with fine hairs.

The large pale - rose, drooping flowers, which pale almost to white on their undersides, are clustered in a dense head at the summit of the stem. Each flower is egg-shaped, the corolla all in one piece, with four small lobes to its mouth. There are eight stamens, the anthers pressed into a compact ring, with their tips touching the style. From the broad end of each anther two curved processes stick out, and almost touch the walls of the corolla.

They contain much nectar, well-known to bee-keepers.

The flowering period extends from July to September.

HEATHER OR LING

Family ERICACEAE   *Calluna vulgaris*

Extending all over Britain, on heaths and moors, and very common in the west.

The Ling is distinguished from the Heaths, on account of its corolla being concealed by the longer, equally coloured calyx leaves, below which are four bracts which resemble a calyx.

It has very tough and wiry stems, bushy at the base, which attain considerable size, especially in the highlands of Scotland.

Its leaves are triangular, very minute and densely packed, overlapping each other in four rows along the branches.

Like the Heaths, its flowers are persistent, and are to be found bleached, but preserving much of their original form, nine or ten months after they have opened. The corolla has not merely four short lobes at the mouth of the bell, but is deeply split into four parts. The anthers are short and contained within the corolla, but the style is long and protrudes.

The flowering period extends from July to September.

WHORTLEBERRY

Family ERICACEAE *Vaccinium myrtillus*

Common in Britain, the Whortleberry may be found growing as abundantly as heather on some of our hills.

It is a shrub, attaining a height of about two feet or more. It has a creeping rootstock from which rise the angular and smooth stems. The leathery, oval leaves are alternate, and when young have a beautiful rosy tint, which is soon exchanged for a dark green, but they get the rosiness back again in the autumn.

The rosy-coloured flowers are pitcher-shaped (*urceolate*), the short neck and mouth of the pitcher being formed by the four or five turned-out lobes of the corolla. Owing to the curving of the short flower-stalks, the flower hangs with its mouth downwards. The simple style occupies the centre of the flower, and its thickened end appears at the mouth of the pitcher, and the stamens are arranged all around. In due time the ovary develops into a succulent blue-black berry.

Flowering from April to June.

MARSH ANDROMEDA

Family ERICACEAE 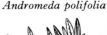   *Andromeda polifolia*

Known also as Wild Rose-
mary, it is one of the diminutive evergreen shrubs of
the Heath family. Though
its distribution is fairly
wide, there are broad
spaces separating the lo-
calities where it may be
found. It extends no
farther north than southern
Scotland.

Seldom more than a
foot in height, the slender,
woody stem at first leans upon the ground, sending
out roots, then ascends. It has half-erect, twiggy
branches and the bark is smooth and brown.

The alternate, glossy, evergreen leaves are
slender, lance-shaped, with their margins rolled
back.

The drooping, rosy-coloured flowers are produced in small clusters at the ends of the branches.
They have red, slender stalks, and consist of four
small sepals and a globular corolla of one piece,
with five turned-out lobes at the mouth. Within
there are two stamens with two-awned anthers
surrounding the simple style.

The fruit is a dry, erect, somewhat globular
capsule, containing numerous oval seeds.

Flowering from May to August.

PRIMROSE

Family PRIMULACEAE   *Primula vulgaris*

Particularly abundant in Britain, in open woods and on hedgerow banks.

It is a perennial, with a thick, fleshy rootstock underground, from which spring the tuft of soft, wrinkled leaves and the crowd of flower-buds at their heart.

The underside of the leaf is covered by a network of stout veins and is softly hairy.

The flowers are on long, slender footstalks of a pinkish colour, all springing from one common stout flower-stem, which is so short as to be hidden among the bases of the leaves.

The flowers have an inflated five-angled calyx, and a funnel-shaped corolla with contracted mouth and broad spreading lobes. The corolla is one and a half inches across, and of a very delicate tint of pale greenish-yellow, the mouth of the tube encircled by five triangular patches of deeper yellow.

The great flowering time is during April and May.

COWSLIP

Family PRIMULACEAE   *Primula veris*

In clayey meadows and pastures throughout England and Ireland the Cowslip is abundant ; in Scotland rare.

It is perennial. From the rootstock a tuft of oblong, pale green and much wrinkled leaves arises ; these are abruptly contracted below the middle. The undersides are strongly veined. The flower-stems spring from the tuft of leaves bearing at the summit an umbel of flowers.

The bell-shaped calyx is toothed, and the funnel-shaped flowers are of a rich yellow colour. They are borne on short pedicels, a number of which spring from the top of the long, stout, velvety stalk, three to six inches high. They have five petals joined together to form a long tube. At the bottom of the tube is the globose ovary, surmounted by a pin-like style, with a spreading stigma at the top. The five stamens are attached to the walls of the tube, in some flowers half-way down, in others at the top.

The flowering period is during April and May.

YELLOW BIRD'S-NEST

Family ERICACEAE   *Monotropa hypopitys*

It occurs locally in woods of pine and beech from mid-Scotland southwards.

It is a perennial saprophyte of the Heath family. Its short, fleshy roots, immersed among decaying leaves, are coated by a web of Mycorrhiza, the fungus that enables it to utilize the products of leaf-decomposition, for the plant has not the power to obtain this benefit direct.

From the rootstock rises the thick and fleshy annual stem, clad in broad, overlapping, pale-yellow scales, the upper part, with its spike of flowers, folded down upon the lower. In the summer the whole plant straightens out, and the drooping, dingy yellow, fragrant flowers stand out horizontally, only the uppermost becoming erect. After fertilization they all become erect. The upper flower differs from the others in having its parts in fives, whilst the lower ones have their parts in fours. The flower is succeeded by a five-valved capsule containing numerous small seeds.

Flowering during the summer.

YELLOW LOOSESTRIFE

Family PRIMULACEAE   *Lysimachia vulgaris*

The Yellow Loosestrife will be found on river banks and in wet, shady places, chiefly in England.

It is a perennial and has a creeping rootstock from which rises an erect, downy stem, three or four feet high. The leaves are broad lance-shaped, with entire edges, stalkless, smooth or downy beneath, but with black glands on the upper surface. They are opposite on the stem, or in whorls of three or four.

From the axils of the upper leaves grow the yellow flowers in cymes, with slender bracts. The flower parts are in fives or sixes. The calyx-lobes are margined with red and have hairy edges. The bell-shaped corolla is deep yellow, dotted with orange inside. The stamens are united below to form a glandular tube and the globose ovary, with its slender style, develops into a round capsule that splits open at the top with five teeth.

The flowers are dimorphic and appear from June to August.

PIMPERNEL

Family PRIMULACEAE   *Anagallis arvensis*

Common everywhere in gardens, fields and waste places. By country-folk it has long enjoyed a reputation as a cheap barometer, in consequence of its habit of closing its petals on the approach of rain. But this is only a reliable indication in the morning, for it invariably closes soon after 2 p.m., rain or shine. Known also as the Scarlet Pimpernel.

It is an annual and has a square stem, which lies along the ground, and sends up many erect branches. The oval leaves are stalkless, the margins without teeth, usually borne in pairs, but occasionally in threes or fours.

The scarlet flowers are produced singly on very long and slender stalks from the axils of the leaves. There is a variety often found with blue flowers.

When the flower has passed, its long stalk curves downwards with the globose seed-vessel, which, when ripe, opens by a fissure all round, so that the upper half falls off and discloses the numerous seeds.

Flowering from May to November.

LESSER PERIWINKLE

Family APOCYNACEAE *Vinca minor*

On woodland banks and shady places the Lesser Periwinkle may be found. It is, perhaps, better known as a garden plant than as a wild flower. It is, however, truly wild in the southern English counties at least, having probably been introduced at an early date and kept the foothold thus obtained. Its favourite position is a woodland bank, which it thickly covers with its dark evergreen leaves.

It is a perennial, with a creeping rootstock and the stem, branching and rooting at the nodes, with short, erect flowering stems. The leaves are opposite, ovate and evergreen.

The solitary blue flowers are borne on short stems produced from the axils of the leaves. The five blue petals are united for half their length to form a tube, the corolla as a whole being salver-shaped.

The plant rarely, if ever, produces seed in this country.

Flowering during April and May, and sparingly throughout the year.

BUTTERWORT

Family LENTIBULARIACEAE   *Pinguicula vulgaris*

May be found in boggy land chiefly in the western hilly districts of England and Scotland, and sparingly as far south as Hants. and Devon.

Interesting, not only on account of its beauty, but for its carnivorous propensities also. The upper surface of the leaves is covered with glandular hairs which secrete a very sticky fluid. Insects, seeds or pollen becoming attached by this fluid, set up an irritation of the leaf, which slowly folds over its lateral edges and secures the exciting object. The leaf then secretes an acid fluid which possesses the power of rapidly dissolving and digesting the offending substance.

It is a perennial, and its thick, stemless leaves form a rosette. From the centre of this cluster rise several purplish stalks, each bearing a solitary violet flower on the recurved tip. The calyx is five-lobed, the lobes unequal. The corolla is two-lipped, unequal, the upper lip having two lobes, the lower three ; there is also a slender spur.

It flowers from May to July.

BUCKBEAN

Family GENTIANACEAE   *Menyanthes trifoliata*

This is another of the very beautiful plants which must be sought in boggy ground. Known also as Beckbean, Bogbean or Marsh Trefoil. It is best appreciated when one alights upon a bog-fringed tarn in a wooded valley and finds the Buckbean rootstocks forming a matted raft stretching half across the tarn, their smooth trefoils shining and setting off the pure whiteness of hundreds of flower-spikes. Such a sight will not readily be forgotten by the flower-lover.

It is an aquatic herb and perennial, with a thick, creeping rootstock. The leaves are alternate, the broad base of their stalks clasping the rootstock. Each leaf is broken up into three smooth, oval leaflets.

The flower-spike bears from three to twelve beautiful blossoms, with five-parted calyx and a funnel-shaped corolla. Externally the corolla is pinkish, but within it is pure white. The five stamens are attached to the corolla tube and are of a reddish colour.

Flowering from May to July.

FIELD BINDWEED

Family CONVOLVULACEAE　　*Convolvulus arvensis*

A common and often troublesome weed in fields and pastures, yet its grace of form and colour make it a general favourite. But it resents the plucking of its delicately fragrant flowers by closing its pink cups almost immediately. It also closes them in wet weather and at night that its nectar may not be reduced in quality.

It is a perennial with a creeping rootstock that branches for many feet underground, taking possession of much soil. The stems are numerous, slender and twining. The leaves are spear-shaped and alternate.

The delicate pink or nearly white flowers are honeyed and scented and are much frequented by long-tongued insects. The sepals are five in number, but the petals are entirely united to form a funnel-shaped corolla ; though the five folds and lobes indicate the origin of the funnel.

The fruit capsule is divided into two cells by a thin partition.

The flowering period is from June to September.

VIPER'S BUGLOSS

Family BORAGINACEAE   *Echium vulgare*

On roadsides and waste places on gravelly and chalky soils the Viper's Bugloss will be found. Abundant in some parts of southern England, becoming rarer in the north. A very stately plant, and prettiest when only one or two flowers are open on each cyme. The recurved cymes are then very short and the unopened flowers packed closely together.

It is an annual or biennial. The unbranched stem attains a height of three feet, its upper part a panicle of red and blue flowers in short cymes. The leaves are strap-shaped, narrowed to the base, long, and rough with stiff hairs, as is the whole plant.

The unopened corollas are purplish-red in colour, when opened bright blue. The parts of the flower are in fives; calyx five-parted, tubular corolla with five-lobed " limb," stamens five, stigma two-lobed. The lobes of the corolla are unequal, and one of the stamens is shorter than the other four, which protrude from the corolla considerably.

Flowering from June to August.

GROMWELL

Family BORAGINACEAE

Lithospermum purpuro-caeruleum

Known also as the Purple Gromwell, this species is rare, and its range is restricted to chalk and limestone soils from Devon to Kent, and in Wales.

It is a perennial, and has a woody, creeping rootstock, and creeping stems about one foot in length ; these do not produce flowers. The slender lance - shaped leaves are scarcely stalked, and are covered with soft bristles which have a bulbous base and lie close to the leaf surface.

The flowering stems are about twice the length of the barren ones, and erect. The flowers are in few-flowered cymes with large leafy bracts, and have very short stalks. The bright blue-purple corolla is salver-shaped with five lobes and five downy folds at the mouth of the tube. It measures three quarters of an inch across. The fruit consists of one or two hard white nutlets of almost globular form.

Flowering in June and July.

SMALL BUGLOSS

Family BORAGINACEAE   *Anchusa arvensis*

Frequently found about cultivated fields upon a light soil, it is an exceedingly bristly—one might almost say prickly—annual.

From a tap-root the rough stem grows to a height of little more than a foot. From the root also grow several stalked leaves, lance-shaped and thickly covered with sharp bristles, as, indeed, is the case with the whole of the plant with the exception of the corolla alone. Each bristle arises from a scaly tuberous base. The stem-leaves are stalkless, oblong and narrow, and partially clasping the stem.

The flowers are in cymes with leafy bracts, almost stalkless. The corolla is tubular, distinctly curved, with five spreading lobes of a brilliant blue colour. The mouth of the tube is closed by five white, hairy scales, one at the base of each lobe. The five stamens are attached to the tube lower down. The four-celled ovary develops into four nutlets.

Flowering in June and July.

Family BORAGINACEAE   *Myosotis scorpioides*

Growing beside or in streams and other wet places, often forming "beds," and abundant throughout the country.

It is perennial. From a creeping rootstock runners are given off, as well as the stout, smooth stem. The leaves are slender, spoon-shaped, smooth and light green ; those from the root stalked, those on the stem stalkless.

The flowers are grouped in cymes, which are at first very short, but as the buds open in succession the stalk lengthens and curves in a manner that has suggested the curl in a scorpion's tail. The name Scorpion-grass is applied to all members of the genus. The calyx is bell-shaped with five teeth and the corolla salver-shaped, the limb divided into five lobes, and the mouth of the tube partly closed by five notched scales. The five stamens and the short style are hidden in the tube. The flowers are light blue with a yellow eye, about a third to half an inch across.

Flowering from May to July.

BITTERSWEET

Family SOLANACEAE   *Solanum dulcamara*

One of the most familiar objects in the hedgerow and moist places is the trailing stem of the Bittersweet or Woody Nightshade.

It is a perennial with a creeping rootstock, from which rise the long, trailing stems that have no means of climbing in the shape of hooks, prickles, etc., but yet by leaning against the stouter hedge plants manage to attain a height of four or five feet. The leaves vary much, the lowest being heart-shaped, the upper more or less spear - shaped. They are very dark green in colour, and all stalked.

The calyx is five-parted; the purple corolla with five lobes, each having at its base two small green tubercles. The five yellow anthers have their edges united so that they form a pyramidal tube, through which the style protrudes. The succeeding berries are egg-shaped and go through a series of colour-changes from green through yellow and orange to a fine red.

Flowering from June to September.

HOUND'S-TONGUE

Family BORAGINACEAE   *Cynoglossum officinale*

By roadsides and waste places the Hound's-tongue may be found. Not a common plant, and yet in some localities it is plentiful enough. Where the Viper's Bugloss is plentiful the Hound's-tongue may be looked for, as the two plants grow in similar situations and sometimes in close proximity.

It is a biennial, and in its first year stores up material for its second year's flowering in a fleshy tapering root. Its root-leaves are nearly a foot long, stalked, oblong or broad lance-shaped.

The flowering stem is two or three feet high, its leaves lance-shaped and stalkless.

The flowers are funnel-shaped, half an inch across, of a dull crimson colour, in forked, lengthening cymes.

When the corolla has fallen, the calyx discloses four flattened nutlets, covered with short, stout, hooked spines, that enable them to cling to fur, feather or textiles. The whole plant gives out a mousy odour. It has narcotic and astringent properties.

The flowers appear in June and July.

HENBANE

Family SOLANACEAE   *Hyoscyamus niger*

Found usually on roadsides and waste places near dwellings, chiefly in the chalk districts. It has long been cultivated for its medicinal properties, and it is highly probable that it is the descendant of these garden plants that we encounter to-day.

It is usually biennial, but sometimes flowers in its first year. It has a stout, round, branching stem from a foot to two feet long ; bearing a scattered covering of long, soft hairs. These are developed more plentifully on the yellowish leaves, and being glandular make the whole plant sticky and invest it with an evil odour.

The radical leaves are oval and stalked. The stem leaves are stalkless, oblong, but cut into several angular lobes ; their bases clasping the stem.

The large, dingy yellow flowers are produced in the axils of the upper leaves. The corolla is funnel-shaped with five broad lobes, with an intricate veining of fine purple lines, occasionally wanting. *It is a poisonous plant which should be handled with care.*

Flowering from June to August.

DEADLY NIGHTSHADE

Family SOLANACEAE   *Atropa belladonna*

The Deadly Nightshade is often found in the neighbourhood of ruins and on the site of former gardens, being probably the descendants of cultivated plants. When it occurs on open wastes or stony places on chalk or limestone soils it may be considered indigenous. Known also as Dwale.

It is perennial. From a thick, fleshy rootstock rise a number of stout annual stems, three or four feet high, forming a bush. The dark-green leaves are egg-shaped. The flowers droop on curved stalks that spring from the axils of the leaves. Calyx, five-parted. Corolla, five-lobed, bell-shaped, dull purple, about an inch across.

The ovary develops into a black berry as big as a cherry, the juice of which is *highly poisonous*. The whole plant has an unpleasant smell and is generally poisonous, and the mere handling of the plant may be attended with inconvenience and some danger.

Its flowering period is from June to August.

YELLOW TOADFLAX

Family SCROPHULARIACEAE *Linaria vulgaris*

Abundant in hedges and waste places all over the British Isles, excepting the Scottish Highlands, where it is rare, the Yellow Toadflax reminds one of the Snapdragon, to which its raceme of bright yellow flowers bears close resemblance ; but the flowers differ from those of the Snapdragon in having a long spur to the corolla.

It is an annual with a slender rootstock, which creeps extensively underground, branching and sending up many stems. The leaves are crowded and of narrow-lanceolate form. The bright yellow flowers form a handsome terminal panicle. The long spur of the corolla is a hollow tube in which nectar is secreted to attract the long-tongued bees, in order that they may fertilize the ovules. Within the closed corolla there are four stamens, sometimes a fifth, and the pistil ending in a notched stigma.

Flowering from June to October.

TOOTHWORT

Family OROBANCHACEAE   *Lathraea squamaria*

A sandy bank that supports a hazel spinney or hedgerow is a suitable situation to look for the Toothwort. Though not common it is generally distributed.

It is perennial and a leafless parasite that consists solely of a fleshy, underground rootstock, and a flower-stem which bears, besides the flowers, a few scales and bracts. The rootstock is branched and the branches are covered with thick scales. It has rootlets which attach themselves by suckers to the rootlets of hazel, elm, etc. The stems are from eight to sixteen inches high, the upper half being covered with solid-looking flowers and their bract-scales. The whole plant is whitish, or flesh-coloured, with a tinge of purple. Each flower is about half an inch long and consists of a two-lipped calyx and a longer purplish two-lipped corolla, with four stamens and a protruded style. The flowers are succeeded by egg-shaped capsules, which open by two valves to distribute the minute seeds.

Flowering during April and May.

KNOTTED FIGWORT

Family SCROPHULARIACEAE *Scrophularia nodosa*

Found in moist, shady places throughout Britain the Figwort gives out a flavour that is nauseous to the human sense of smell, but to flies and wasps, by which it is fertilized, it is no doubt suggestive of carrion.

It is perennial and has a knotted, tuberous root-stock, a four-angled stem, with opposite, pointed, egg-shaped, stalked leaves, their edges sharply toothed, and the teeth themselves edged with secondary teeth. The stem varies from one to three feet high and is unbranched.

The flowers are arranged in cymes. Calyx five-parted, a corolla-tube swollen at the lower part, the mouth cut into five unequal lobes. The colour of the corolla is either green or brownish. The stigmas are ripe before the anthers, a condition entirely the opposite of many plants, but the object is the same in each case. Flies that have already visited an older flower drop a little of the pollen on the stigmas of the younger blossom, thus securing cross-fertilization.

Flowering from July to October.

FOXGLOVE

Family SCROPHULARIACEAE   *Digitalis purpurea*

One of the best-known flowers of the countryside, and familiar for the masses of purple blossoms it presents on dry wastes and woodland slopes throughout Britain.

It is biennial or perennial. The soft downy leaves are minutely wrinkled above, whilst below the network of ribs and nervures stand out in bold relief. Those from the root only are stalked ; those on the stem are alternate, and gradually pass into bracts, from the axils of which the large, broadly tubular flowers droop. The corolla is usually bright purple, speckled and spotted within, but sometimes it occurs orange or yellow, more frequently white. The four stamens are in two pairs. The stigma is not mature until the pollen has been shed. The hairs in the corolla mouth prevent the pollen falling out, as well as keeping out minute nectar stealers. Fertilization is effected by humblebees, their hairy bodies brush up the pollen and convey it to the stigma of an older flower.

Flowering from June to September.

YELLOW RATTLE

Family SCROPHULARIACEAE   *Rhinanthus minor*

In meadows and pastures the Yellow Rattle is abundant, where it is parasitical upon the roots of other plants. The yellow flowers render it very conspicuous, and its identity is readily established by the light-green inflated calyx.

It is an annual with a branched, fibrous root which attaches itself to the living roots of grasses and other plants by means of slightly enlarged suckers. The stem is square; the leaves distant, opposite, stalkless, narrow, the edges deeply toothed. The flowers are borne in a loose, leafy spike. The calyx is a light-green bladder with flattened sides and a four-toothed mouth. The corolla is yellow, tubular, two-lipped; the upper lip is arched over, somewhat in the form of a knight's casque, with two blue lobes; the lower lip spread outward, with three lobes. There are four stamens concealed within the upper lip; the anthers are blue and hairy.

The flowers will be found from May to August.

RED BARTSIA

Family SCROPHULARIACEAE   *Odontites verna*

Generally distributed over Britain in fields and waste places.

It is an annual and parasitic upon the roots of other plants. In general appearance it does not differ greatly from the Yellow Rattle, though it lacks the prominent bladders.

The stem is erect, branching and downy, rising to about a foot high. The leaves are lanceolate in form and are toothed. The flowers are borne in one-sided spikes. The pink or dull purple corolla is downy. The whole plant in fact is tinged with purple and downy. Nectar is secreted at the base of the corolla-tube. The anthers are hairy and hang close together above the mouth of the tube ; the filaments being so bent as to allow room for the passage of a bee's proboscis in its search for nectar. The anthers ripen after the stigma, which first comes into a prominent position, and gets fertilized with pollen brought from an older flower.

Flowering from June to August.

GIPSYWORT

Family LABIATAE   *Lycopus europaeus*

Around the margins of ponds, along the banks of ditches and streams, the Gipsywort may often be found amongst the crowded vegetation. It is generally distributed in England and Ireland, less frequent in Scotland. But it is the leaves more than the small flowers that are likely first to attract attention.

It is a perennial with a creeping rootstock which sends out runners. The stem is square and rises to about three feet high. The leaves are opposite, elliptical, with very brief stalks, and their margins are deeply cut.

The small, stalkless flowers are produced in dense whorls from the axils of the leaves. Both calyx and corolla are bell-shaped. The corolla is bluish-white dotted with purple, which gives a pinkish effect. There are four stamens, of which two are imperfect, the perfect ones keeping away from the two-lobed style and discharging their pollen before the stigmas are mature.

Flowering from June to September.

GERMANDER SPEEDWELL

Family SCROPHULARIACEAE *Veronica chamaedrys*

In woods, pastures, hedge-banks and roadsides this species is generally distributed all over Britain, and often shows to greatest advantage when growing in a mass on some sloping bank, where its bright blue flowers are very attractive.

It is a perennial with stems about a foot long, which at first creep and root, then ascend. The stalkless leaves are opposite and are of oval form, with edges coarsely toothed. The racemes of flowers are usually in pairs. The bright blue corolla is tubular for half its length, the upper portion divided into four spreading lobes, of which the upper and lower are usually longer than the lateral pair. The two stamens are attached within the corolla-tube just below the upper lobe, and the anthers and stigma protrude beyond the mouth of the tube. The seed-vessel is a two-celled, flattened, heart-shaped capsule.

One of the names for the flower is Cat's-eye, and many continue to call it Forget-me-not.

Flowering in May and June.

GROUND IVY

Family L*ABIATAE*   *Glechoma hederacea*

The Ground Ivy will
be found trailing
among the grass of the
copse and hedgebank.
It is very abundant in
Britain and one of the
earliest of flowers to
appear in spring. It
has not the remotest
relationship with the
real Ivy. It is also
known as Ale-hoof and
Tun-hoof, being for-
merly used in brewing
owing to its tonic
bitterness.

It is a perennial with
a slender, square stem
which creeps along the
ground, and wherever it puts forth a pair of
leaves it sends down a tuft of fibrous roots also.
The leaves are roundish, kidney-shaped, and
deeply round-toothed on the margin.

The purple-blue flowers are in whorls of three
to six, borne in the axils of leaf-like bracts. The
corolla-tube is long, slender at the base, afterwards dilating, the lower lip heart-shaped and
flat. The flowers are dimorphic, some being
large and perfect, others small and devoid of
stamens.

Flowering from March to June.

WATER MINT

In wet and marshy wastes, and on the edges of streams, the Water Mint may be found. Abundant in Britain generally, but becoming rare in the north of Scotland.

It is a perennial with a creeping rootstock, which gives off runners freely. It has square stems, rising to a height of from twelve to eighteen inches, and much branched. The leaves are stalked, opposite, hairy and ovate in form, the edges indented with rounded teeth.

The flowers, individually, are small, but rendered more conspicuous by being borne in dense, terminal whorls, the whorls being often so many, and so close together, as to form long spikes of bloom. Occasionally additional whorls spring from the axils of the upper leaves. The tubular corolla has five lobes which form two unequal lips to the mouth of the tube. The colour of the flowers varies from lilac to purple.

Flowering in August and September.

Family LABIATAE   *Prunella vulgaris*

Commonest by the wayside and in damp pastures, and abundant throughout Britain.

It is a perennial with a creeping rootstock, with ascending flowering branches, three to twelve inches high. The stem is square and the stalked leaves are long, oval in shape, with either toothed or entire margins. Both stem and leaves are more or less hairy.

The bracts of the flower-spike have purple edges. The lipped flowers are mostly purple, sometimes white or crimson. There are four stamens. There is a peculiarity in the form of the stamens worth noting. The filament branches at the tip, and one branch bears the anthers whilst the other is pressed against the upper lip. The flowers are dimorphic, large and small—the large perfect, the small having no anthers.

The plant is also known as Carpenter's Herb, Hook-heal, Sickle-wort and Prunella. In olden days it was considered one of the most useful medicines for inward and outward wounds.

Flowering from July to September.

COMMON HEMP NETTLE

Family LABIATAE   *Galeopsis tetrahit*

The Common Hemp Nettle may be looked for round about cultivated ground and waste places generally.

It is an annual, and its square, bristly stems rise to a height of about three feet. The stems are much swollen beneath the nodes, whence the leaves and branches are given off. The long-stalked, opposite leaves are large, ovate, pointed and very coarsely toothed.

The rosy-purple or white flowers are borne in dense whorls around the upper part of the stem, with leafy bracts beneath them. The five teeth of the bell-shaped calyx are very long, straight and awl-shaped. The corolla-tube is straight, with a divided throat; the upper lip egg-shaped and arched, the lower three-lobed, with erect teeth where the lobes unite.

The Hemp Nettle frequently gets confused with the Dead Nettle on account of the superficial resemblance of their foliage, and the similar squareness of their stems and opposite branches.

Flowering from July to September.

RED DEAD-NETTLE

Family LABIATAE   *Lamium purpureum*

May be found in cultivated and waste places, and common throughout Britain, especially as a garden weed.

It is an annual with square stems rising from a few inches to a foot in height.

The long-stalked lower leaves are small, but the upper leaves ~~are~~ all shortly stalked, heart-shaped and with toothed edges.

The purplish-red flowers are borne on the upper part of the stem in distinct whorls. The corolla has a short tube, and the two long lips are distended, the upper vaulted, the lower with three lobes. The calyx is tubular with five teeth.

It is entirely unrelated to the Stinging Nettles, and apart from the resemblance in the form of the leaves there is little likeness between them. In the absence of flowers, the difference may be quickly seen by cutting the stems across. It will be found that the stem of the Red Dead-nettle is square and tubular, that of the Stinging Nettle is solid and round.

Flowering from April to October.

YELLOW ARCHANGEL

Family LABIATAE   *Galeobdolon luteum*

The Yellow Archangel must be sought for in copse, bushy hedgerow and shady places. Known also as Weasel-snout, it is really one of the Dead-nettles.

It is a perennial, and the plant increases partly by means of runners from the rootstock. The square flowering stem rises to about two feet high, whilst the others which do not bear flowers, run along the ground. The leaves are opposite, oval and stalked, with rounded teeth, one to two inches long.

The bright yellow flowers are in distinct whorls, from six to ten in each, springing from the axils of the leaves. The corolla has a short tube, and the two long lips are distended, the upper vaulted, the lower three-lobed and spotted with brown. The stamens and style follow the curvature of the upper lip, against which they lie.

The flowering period is during May and June.

BUGLE

Family LABIATAE   *Ajuga reptans*

Common in springtime in woodland and field, and on the waste
places by the roadside.

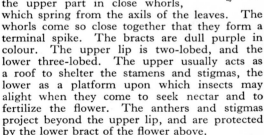

It is a perennial with a stout,
short, creeping rootstock, from
which runners are sent out and
these rooting. The square flowering stems attain a height of from
six to twelve inches. The leaves
from the root have long stalks ;
those from the stems are stalkless.

The flowering stems are erect,
and the blue flowers are borne on
the upper part in close whorls,
which spring from the axils of the leaves. The
whorls come so close together that they form a
terminal spike. The bracts are dull purple in
colour. The upper lip is two-lobed, and the
lower three-lobed. The upper usually acts as
a roof to shelter the stamens and stigmas, the
lower as a platform upon which insects may
alight when they come to seek nectar and to
fertilize the flower. The anthers and stigmas
project beyond the upper lip, and are protected
by the lower bract of the flower above.

When the flower opens the two lobes (stigmas)
of the style are already mature and fit for
receiving pollen brought from an older flower,
anthers not shedding their pollen until the stigmas
have been fertilized.

Flowering from April to July.

SEA LAVENDER

Family PLUMBAGINACEAE   *Limonium vulgare*

On sand-dunes by the sea, and on muddy sea-shores, the Sea Lavender may often be seen covering great tracts with continuous sheets of purple bloom, reminding one of the purple heath on the moorlands and hills.

It is a perennial with a woody, creeping and branching rootstock, sending up many angular flower stems from twelve to eighteen inches high, which are considerably branched in the upper part, and nearly every branch bears flowers. All the leaves spring directly from the rootstock, and are lance-shaped, with long stalks and marked with one prominent rib ; the tip often ends in a minute hard point.

The green calyx has a distinctly purple tinge, and there is a little tooth between the lobes. The flowers are coloured bluish-purple and are of regular shape, their parts in fives, with short foot-stalks, grouped in cymes and arranged in panicles.

Flowering from July to November.

THRIFT

Family PLUMBAGINACEAE   *Armeria maritima*

The natural habitat of the Thrift is on the rocks and cliffs of the sea-shore or the rocky sides of high mountains. Known also as Sea Pink.

It is a perennial with a long, thick, woody and much - branched root-stock. Every branch ends in a bundle of bright green grass-like leaves that are truly linear. From the centre of the leaf - bundle rises the smooth, softly - hairy flower stem, six to nine inches high, ending in a half - round bunch of flowers, with its involucre of thin, tough scales. The lowest of these scales form a purplish sheath, half an inch long, round the stalk. The individual pale, rosy flowers are separately stalked. The calyx is funnel-shaped with five lobes, and the corolla consists of five-clawed petals. There are five yellow anthers, and the ovary bears five long, thread-like stigmas. The central flower in each head opens first, and the stamens mature before the stigmas.

Flowering from April to October.

LAMB'S-TONGUE PLANTAIN

Family PLANTAGINACEAE   *Plantago media*

Abundant in England and the south of Scotland it will be found in dry pastures and waste places, chiefly on limestone soils. Although the Plantains are among the despised of our wild flowers, the Lamb's-tongue in flower on a bank is really a thing of beauty.

It is a perennial. There is no stem, the elliptic-shaped leaves all springing from the stout rootstock, closely spreading on the ground, and characterized by having strongly developed, parallel ribs on their under surface.

The flowers are borne on tall, dense, cylindrical spikes, which rise from the axils of the leaves. Each blossom consists of four persistent sepals, a salver-shaped corolla with four lobes, between which are fixed the four stamens surrounding the long, simple and hairy style. The purple stamens form the most conspicuous feature of the flower-spike.

The flowering period is from June to October.

ANNUAL SEABLITE

Family CHENOPODIACEAE   *Suaeda maritima*

Where there are salt-marshes, muddy or sandy shores on most parts of our coasts, there will be little difficulty in finding the Annual Seablite.

It is an annual, and rather untidy in its growth. Its erect, leafy stems rise to a height of two feet, others, as also the long branches, are half-erect or trailing on the ground. The long, fleshy leaves are half-cylindrical, with an acute tip and tapering at the base ; though arranged alternately they are crowded on the branches.

The small, green flowers are inconspicuous and partially hidden by the leaves. They may be solitary, but are usually in threes or fives. They consist of a five-parted calyx, no corolla and five stamens and a pistil. The fruit is bladder-like, enclosing a brownish-black, beaked seed.

The flowering period is from July to October.

BLOOD-VEINED DOCK

Family POLYGONACEAE   *Rumex sanguineus*

A widespread perennial of roadside wastes, ditches and pastures.

There are two superficially different forms : one which supplies the distinctive name has the veins of the leaf coloured dark crimson, and the remainder of the leaf, more or less suffused with dark red ; in the other, sometimes called *R. viridis*, the whole leaf is uniformly green. The red-veined form is the rarer of the two.

When in flower or fruiting it may attain a height of four feet, the slender stem with few or no branches. The leaves are oval or oblong, lance-shaped, slightly wavy, the root-leaves with a rounded or heart-shaped base.

The flower-spikes are usually leafless except at the base. The flowers, though produced in abundance, are very small and in whorls.

The fruiting sepals are oblong, the upper one with a large, smooth tubercle.

The flowering period is during July and August.

COMMON SORREL

Family POLYGONACEAE   *Rumex acetosa*

Abundant throughout the country in moist meadows, pastures and woods.

Separated from the Docks under the name of Sorrel to indicate the sourness of their foliage. Their leafing does not suggest any close affinity with the Docks, though their flowering might raise a suspicion, turned to a certainty by close examination.

It is a perennial and has a slender, tufted rootstock, with a rosette of long-stalked, arrow - shaped leaves. The slender flowering stem rises to a height of a foot or two, with stalkless leaves whose bases clasp the stem. The stipules are brown. From the axils of the upper leaves long, slim, flowering branches are produced, with the small flowers in whorls, as in the larger Docks. Male flowers appear on one plant and female flowers on another ; the male whorls are more densely flowered and less strongly tinged with red than in the females.

Flowering from May to August.

CROWBERRY

Family EMPETRACEAE   *Empetrum nigrum*

Though it may be described as a moorland plant, we may find it in wet peat-bogs or amongst dry rocks, on bare sand or among the heath ; but it must have light and air without stint. Plentiful in the Highlands of Scotland, it extends south as far as Devon and Dorset.

It is a low, heath-like trailing shrub. From the short stem which lies upon the ground and roots from its lower surface, slender, wiry branches spread and trail, densely clothed with short-stalked elliptical leaves of the heath type. They are only about one-third of an inch long, and evergreen. They turn red when old.

The purple-red flowers are very minute, and are produced from the axils of the leaves near the ends of the shoots.

The edible fruits are little cherry-like drupes, usually black, containing from one to nine seeds. They have little flavour. In combination with alum they yield a dingy purple dye.

Known also as Crakeberry and Black-berried Heath.

Flowering in the Spring.

WILD HOP

Family CANNABIACEAE   *Humulus lupulus*

May not infrequently be found in the copse and hedgerow, especially in the south of England.

It is a perennial with a thick, branching rootstock from which are produced several long, thin and rough twining stems which tightly clasp the nearest small tree or shrub, twining with the sun, Convolvulus like, as it grows. The leaves are lobed and coarsely toothed, and very rough. It is termed by botanists a *diœcious* plant, because staminate flowers are produced by one individual, and pistillate only by another, making cross-fertilization imperative. The small staminate flowers are produced from the axils of the leaves in long, drooping panicles. Each pistillate flower has a sepal, an ovary and two long, purple stigmas. Two of these flowers are produced in the axil of a green concave bract. A number of these bracts are united into a dense spike, which develops into a cone-like head of yellow scales. The true fruit is a little nut, enclosed in the sepal under the bracts.

Flowering in July and August.

GREAT REED MACE

Family TYPHACEAE   *Typha latifolia*

Abundant in Britain, and will be found growing in lakes, ponds and on the banks of rivers.

It is a perennial with a creeping rootstock, with erect, naked, reed-like stems rising to a height of six or seven feet. The leaves are long, narrow and grass-like, their bases sheathing the stem. The stamens and pistils are produced in separate flowers, but upon the same plant. They have no perianth other than a few slender hairs. The yellow staminate flowers occupy the upper portion of the spike or " mace," and each one consists simply of several stamens joined together, the anthers opening along their sides. The closely packed pistillate flowers forming the " mace " consist of a stalked ovary, with a slender style and a one-sided, narrow stigma, and enveloped in tufts of soft, brownish hairs.

It has become a general error to call this plant the Bulrush, a name which rightly belongs to *Scirpus lacustris*, and every autumn large numbers are sold as Bulrushes.

Flowering in July and August.

CUCKOO-PINT

Family ARACEAE

Arum maculatum

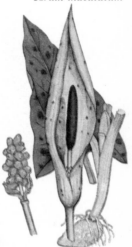

The Cuckoo-pint is to be found in woods and hedgebanks and is plentiful throughout the country. Known also as Lords - and - Ladies, Cuckoo - pintle, Wake-robin, etc.

About a foot below the surface of the ground is the tuberous root-stock, from which arise, in March, the arrow-shaped leaves, often spotted with black or purple. From the middle of these leaves, in April, rises the flower-stalk, bearing an enormous pale-green bract-leaf. It unrolls and then resembles a monk's cowl, and discloses a purplish cylindrical column. The green envelope is called a spathe, and is not a flower. The small flowers are in great number, arranged round the lower part of the central column, called the spadix. The lower third of the spathe is marked off by a slight constriction, where the flowers will be found in four series.

The spathe and spadix wither, but the ovaries develop into bright red berries, in a short spike, on a naked peduncle.

EARLY PURPLE ORCHIS

Family ORCHIDACEAE   *Orchis mascula*

May be found in meadows, pastures and woodlands throughout the British Isles, and is the commonest as well as the earliest of our native Orchids.

It is a perennial with a rootstock forming two tubers which are egg-shaped and close to the stem. The leaves are narrow-oblong with a blunt point, more or less spotted with purple-black, which may be in broad patches or reduced to small spots.

The flower-stem varies in height from six to eighteen inches, ending in a spike of from six to thirty flowers of a red-purple colour. The sepals are turned upwards. The lip is marked with small spots of dark purple and divided into three lobes. The stout, blunt spur is longer than the ovary. The flowers vary in colour, some being almost white; and a similar irregularity in different plants is found in their odour, varying as scarcely perceptible, pleasantly fragrant or disgusting.

The flowering period is from April to June.

BEE ORCHIS

Family ORCHIDACEAE   *Ophrys apifera*

The Bee Orchis is the best known from its appearance, often in great numbers on the slopes of the chalk and limestone hills; sometimes also in pastures and copses.

The two tubers are more or less oval. The lower leaves are short, lance-shaped, clasping the stem; the stem-leaves are narrower. The flower-stem varies from four to eighteen inches in height. There are usually four to six flowers on a spike, but only two or three are open at one time. There is a large bract at the base of each flower. The sepals are pink, with a greenish line down the middle; but the petals are small, downy, purple or green. The lip has five lobes. The ground colour of the lip is deep yellow, overlaid with patches of purple-brown. The distribution of the yellow and brown produces varied patterns. Many attempts have been made to explain the likeness of the flower to a bee, and much divergence of opinion still exists.

Flowering in June and July.

Family ORCHIDACEAE   *Dactylorchis maculata*

Occurs commonly in damp places in all parts of the country, in meadows, pastures and open woods, on stiff soils and on chalk downs.

It has a tuber, more or less flattened, the lower part dividing into thick, finger-like lobes which run downwards. Other fleshy roots spread out from above the tubers. These will be found webbed with the delicate filaments of the root fungus. The slender, straight stem varies in height from six inches to two feet, ending in a dense spike of pale purple flowers. The leaves are usually spotted with dark purple : the lowest oval, short and blunt ; the upper narrow and sharply pointed. Both sepals and petals are pale purple. The lip is marked with dots of deeper purple and is cut into three lobes. The usually straight spur is nearly as long as the ovary. The lines and dots on the lip vary greatly in strength of colour.

Flowering from June—occasionally in May—to as late as August.

PYRAMIDAL ORCHIS

Family ORCHIDACEAE   *Anacamptis pyramidalis*

One of the prettiest of our Orchids, it is found chiefly on chalk and limestone soils in England ; more rarely in Scotland and Ireland. On some of the southern chalk hills it occurs in great abundance.

The tubers are roundish, and the slender, erect stem measures from six inches to two feet. The unspotted leaves are narrow lance-shaped ; the lower partially, and the upper entirely clasping the stem. When the lowest crimson-purple flowers open the spike is distinctly pyramidal in form ; but when the upper blossoms expand, it becomes more oblong. The colour effect is heightened by the purple tint of the long bract below each flower. The petals and the upper sepal form a pointed hood and the side sepals spread outwards. The lip is broad, cut into three oblong lobes. The slender spur is longer than the ovary. A peculiar odour is given off which appears to vary or to strike different noses as pleasant or unpleasant.

The flowering period is from June to August.

YELLOW FLAG

Family IRIDACEAE

Iris pseudacorus

Fringing our rivers, ditches and lakes the Yellow Iris will be found abundantly throughout Britain.

The thick, horizontal, creeping rootstock has numerous fibres, and the stem rises to a height of two feet. The leaves are stiff, erect and sharp-edged, so much so that they may cut the hands of a careless gatherer, and are of a pale green colour.

There are two or three large, erect, bright yellow flowers which proceed from a sheathing bract. The parts of the flower are in threes, but the sepals are more petal-like than the petals, and so are the styles. The sepals are the most striking organs ; they are broad and reflexed. The petals are narrow, erect or curved towards the centre of the flower. The broad arching style is spread out and coloured like a petal, with the stigmatic surface near the upturned tips. Beneath this arching style lies the anther, similarly curved and opening away from the stigma.

Flowering in May and continuing until late in July.

AUTUMN CROCUS

Family IRIDACEAE   *Crocus nudiflorus*

In meadows and pastures of the English midlands the Autumn Crocus may be found.

The rootstock consists of a solid corm, clothed in a thin coat of straight, brown fibres. From this corm arises in September a solitary flower-bud, wrapped in a delicate spathe, without any stem; neither are there at this time any leaves. The lower portion of the flower is a long silky tube which dilates upwards and divides into six bright purple lobes, which show no distinction between sepals and petals, except that three are outer in the bud and three inner. There are three stamens. The ovary is down below, close to the corm, and the thread-like style divides into three orange-coloured stigmas. The pale-orange anthers stand on the same level as the stigmas. In the following March the leaves appear above ground to provide sufficient material to form a new corm and feed the seed capsule. The leaves wither, the capsule opens and the seeds scatter

Flowering in September and October.

WILD DAFFODIL

Family AMARYLLIDACEAE

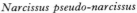

Narcissus pseudo-narcissus

The Daffodil as a wild plant in England is extremely local, but where it occurs it is usually in great profusion.

The rootstock is in the form of a bulb, and the somewhat flattened flower-scape is leafless, though the flower is first enveloped in a dry, skin-like spathe or bract. The few linear leaves spring directly from the rootstock; they are nearly flat and of a glaucous, blue-green colour. They enlarge greatly after flowering.

Only one flower appears on the scape, and consists of a perianth of six coloured floral leaves, without distinction between sepals and petals, and attached above the ovary. The perianth segments are a clear pale yellow, but from the centre is produced a long tubular crown of a golden hue, with an uneven toothed margin. Within this tube are the six stamens, and the long style with its three-lobed stigma. The ovary is egg-shaped or round and is three-celled.

Flowering in March and April.

BLUEBELL OR WILD HYACINTH

Family LILIACEAE   *Endymion non-scriptus*

Abundant in woods, hedges and shady places throughout Britain.

The rootstock consists of a white, juicy roundish bulb about an inch in diameter. In spring its leaves break through the earth and lay in rosette fashion close to the surface, leaving a circular tube through which the spike of pale unopened buds rises to a height of about a foot. The growing leaves are linear, and before the plant has done flowering they may reach the length of a foot or more, whilst the flower-stalk is nearly as long again, bearing a terminal one-sided raceme of drooping blue flowers.

The flower is bell-shaped, showing no distinction between calyx and corolla, and therefore called a perianth. It consists of six floral leaves, joined at their bases, the free portions curling back disclosing the six yellow anthers. The ovary is surmounted by the thread-like style, ending in a minute stigma.

Flowering in April and May.

SNOWDROP

Family AMARYLLIDACEAE   *Galanthus nivalis*

Although it may be found thoroughly naturalized and quite wild in orchards, copses and meadows, it is generally agreed that the Snowdrop is not indigenous to this country.

Its rootstock takes the form of a little brown bulb, and from this appears, in the very earliest days of the year, often when the ground is covered with snow, a solitary pair of long, straight-sided, narrow leaves of a glaucous or sea-green colour, and slightly keeled on the outer surface. A little later there comes up direct from the bulb an unbranched flower-stem or scape, bearing a large bract or spathe, from which issues the solitary flower on a thin, bending stalk.

The three sepals are pure white, and the three smaller petals are also white, but with a patch of green near the upper edge of each. There are six stamens and a slender style. The flower is honeyed and scented, and remains open from about ten till four. The ovary is inferior.

Flowering from January to March.

INDEX

Achillea millefolium, 135
Adonis annua, 20
ADOXACEAE, 117
Adoxa moschatellina, 117
Aethusa cynapium, 107
Agrimonia eupatoria, 100
Agrimony, 100
—, Hemp, 128
Agrostemma githago, 59
Ajuga reptans, 197
Alchemilla vulgaris, 96
Alliaria petiolata, 38
Althaea officinalis, 65
AMARYLLIDACEAE, 214, 216
Anacamptis pyramidalis, 211
Anagallis arvensis, 170
Anchusa arvensis, 177
Andromeda, Marsh, 165
— *polifolia*, 165
Anemone nemorosa, 19
—, Wood, 19
Angelica, 109
— *sylvestris*, 109
Anthemis arvensis, 134
Anthriscus sylvestris, 111
Anthyllis vulneraria, 86
APOCYNACEAE, 171
Apium graveolens, 106
Apple, Crab, 99
Aquilegia vulgaris, 27
ARACEAE, 207
ARALIACEAE, 118

Archangel, Yellow, 196
Arctium minus, 141
Armeria maritima, 199
Artemisia vulgaris, 137
Arum maculatum, 207
Aster, Sea, 130
— *tripolium*, 130
Atropa belladonna, 182
Avens, Wood, 89

Barberry, 28
Bartsia, Red, 188
Bedstraw, Hedge, 121
—, Lady's, 124
Bell, Canterbury, 158
Bellflower, Ivy-leaved, 160
—, Nettle-leaved, 158
Bellis perennis, 129
BERBERIDACEAE, 28
Berberis vulgaris, 28
Bindweed, Field, 174
Bird's-nest, Yellow, 168
Bittersweet, 179
Blackberry, 91
Bluebell, 215
BORAGINACEAE, 175–178, 180
Bramble, 91
Brandy-bottle, 29
Broom, 72
Bryonia dioica, 104
Bryony, White, 104
Buckbean, 173
Bugle, 197

Bugloss, Small, 177
—, Viper's, 175
Burdock, Lesser, 141
Burnet, Salad, 97
Butterbur, 139
Buttercup, 22
Butterwort, 172

Cakile maritima, 46
Calluna vulgaris, 163
Caltha palustris, 26
Cammock, 78
Campanula rotundifolia, 159
— *trachelium*, 158
CAMPANULACEAE, 155, 157–161
Campion, Bladder, 54
—, Red, 55
CANNABIACEAE, 205
CAPRIFOLIACEAE, 119
Capsella bursa-pastoris, 43
Cardamine pratensis, 35
Carduus nutans, 145
Carpenter's Herb, 193
Carrot, Wild, 106
CARYOPHYLLACEAE 49, 52–60, 62, 63
Catch-flies, 54
Cat's-ear, Long-rooted, 150
Cat's-eye, 190
Celandine, Greater, 33
—, Lesser, 23
Celery, Wild, 106
Centaurea scabiosa, 146
Centranthus ruber, 122
Cerastium holosteoides, 62

Chamaenerion angustifolium, 102
Chamomile, Corn, 134
Charlock, 39
Chelidonium majus, 33
CHENOPODIACEAE, 201
Chickweed, Common Mouse-ear, 62
Chicory, 153
Chrysanthemum leucanthemum, 131
Chrysanthemum vulgare, 136
Cichorium intybus, 153
Cinquefoil, 95
Circaea lutetiana, 101
Cirsium vulgare, 143
CISTACEAE, 47
Cleavers, 120
Clematis vitalba, 18
Clover, Red, 82
Cochlearia officinalis, 40
Cockle, Corn, 59
Columbine, 27
Coltsfoot, 138
COMPOSITAE, 127–154, 156
Conium maculatum, 115
Conopodium majus, 112
CONVOLVULACEAE, 174
Convolvulus arvensis, 174
Cowslip, 167
Crakeberry, 204
Crambe maritima, 44
Crane's-bill Dove's-foot, 68
CRASSULACEAE, 105

Cress, Water, 34
Crocus, Autumn, 213
Crocus nudiflorus, 213
Crowberry, 204
Crowfoot, Water, 21
CRUCIFERAE, 34, 35, 37–44, 46
Cuckoo-pint, 207
— -pintle, 207
CUCURBITACEAE, 104
Cynoglossum officinale, 180

Dactylorchis maculata, 210
Daffodil, Wild, 214
Daisy, 129
—, Ox-eye, 131
Dandelion, 151
Daucus carota, 114
Dead-nettle, Red, 195
Dianthus deltoides, 49
Digitalis purpurea, 186
DIPSACACEAE, 123, 126
Dipsacus fullonum, 123
Dock, Blood-veined, 202
Dockorenes, 156
Dropwort, Water, 108
Dwale, 182

Earth-nut, 112
Echium vulgare, 175
EMPETRACEAE, 204
Empetrum nigrum, 204
Endymion non-scriptus, 215
Erica tetralix, 162
ERICACEAE, 162–165, 168
Erodium cicutarium, 69

Erysimum cheiranthoides, 37
Eupatorium cannabinum, 128

Figwort, Knotted, 185
Filipendula ulmaria, 90
Flag, Yellow, 212
Flax, Common, 61
Fleabane, Common, 132
Forget-me-not, 178
Foxglove, 186
Fragaria vesca, 94
Fumaria officinalis, 36
FUMARIACEAE, 36
Fumitory, 36
Furze, 74

Galanthus nivalis, 216
Galeobdolon luteum, 196
Galeopsis tetrahit, 194
Galium aparine, 120
— *mollugo*, 121
— *odoratum*, 125
— *verum*, 124
Genista anglica, 75
GENTIANACEAE, 173
GERANIACEAE, 68, 69, 71
Geranium molle, 68
Geum urbanum, 89
Gipsywort, 189
Glaucium flavum, 32
Glechoma hederacea, 191
Globe Flower, 24
Glossary, 11
Goat's-beard, 148
Golden Rod, 127
Goose Grass, 120

Gowan, 131
Gromwell, 176
Groundsel, 140

Hard-heads, 146
Harebell, 159
Hawkweed, 154
Heath, Black-berried, 204
—, Cross-leaved, 162
Heather, 163
Hedera helix, 118
Helianthemum chamaecistus, 47
Helleborus foetidus, 25
Hemlock, 115
Henbane, 181
Heracleum sphondylium, 110
Hieracium perpropinquum, 154
Hippocrepis comosa, 80
Hog-weed, 110
Honeysuckle, 119
Honkenya peploides, 53
Hook-heal, 193
Hop, Wild, 205
Horse-Gowan, 131
Hound's-tongue, 180
Humulus lupulus, 205
Hyacinth, Wild, 215
Hyoscyamus niger, 181
HYPERICACEAE, 67
Hypericum perforatum, 67
Hypochoeris radicata, 150

Introduction, 7
IRIDACEAE, 212, 213
Iris pseudacorus, 212
Isatis tinctoria, 41

Ivy, 118
—, Ground, 191

Jack-by-the-Hedge, 38
Jasione montana, 157

Kale, Sea, 44
King-cup, 26
Knautia arvensis, 126

LABIATAE, 189, 191–197
Lady's Mantle, 96
— Slipper, 76
— Smock, 35
Lamium purpureum, 195
Lapsana communis, 156
Lathraea squamaria, 184
Lathyrus nissolia, 88
— *pratensis*, 87
Lavatera arborea, 64
Lavender, Sea, 198
Legousia hybrida, 161
LEGUMINOSAE, 72–88
LENTIBULARIACEAE, 172
Lettuce, Wall, 149
LILIACEAE, 215
Limonium vulgare, 198
LINACEAE, 61
Linaria vulgaris, 183
Ling, 163
Linum usitatissimum, 61
Lithospermum purpurocaeruleum, 176
Lonicera periclymenum, 119
Loosestrife, Purple, 103
—, Yellow, 169
LORANTHACEAE, 116
Lords and Ladies, 207

Lotus corniculatus, 76
Lucerne, 73
Luckan Gowan, 20
Lychnis flos-cuculi, 58
Lycopus europaeus, 189
Lysimachia vulgaris, 169
LYTHRACEAE, 103
Lythrum salicaria, 103

Mace, Great Reed, 206
Mallow, Common, 70
—, Marsh, 65
—, Tree, 64
Malus sylvestris, 99
Malva sylvestris, 70
MALVACEAE, 64, 65,
  70
Marigold, Marsh, 26
Mayweed, Scentless, 133
Meadow-rue, 17
— -sweet, 90
Meconopsis cambrica, 31
Medicago sativa, 73
Melilot, Tall, 79
Melilotus altissima, 79
Mentha aquatica, 192
Menyanthes trifoliata, 173
Mignonette, Wild, 45
Milkwort, 48
Mint, Water, 192
Mistletoe, 116
Monotropa hypopitys, 168
Moschatel, 117
Mugwort, 137
Mustard, Garlic, 38
—, Mithridate, 42
—, Treacle, 37
—, Wild, 39
Mycelis muralis, 149

Myosotis scorpioides, 178

Narcissus pseudo-narcissus,
  214
Navelwort, 105
Needle-whin, 75
Nettle, Common Hemp,
  194
Nightshade, Deadly, 182
—, Enchanter's, 101
—, Woody, 179
Nipplewort, 156
Nuphar lutea, 29
NYMPHAEACEAE, 29

Odontites verna, 188
Oenanthe fistulosa, 108
Old Man's Beard, 18
ONAGRACEAE, 101,
  102
Onobrychis viciifolia, 81
Ononis spinosa, 78
Ophrys apifera, 209
ORCHIDACEAE, 208–
  211
Orchis, Bee, 209
—, Early Purple, 208
— *mascula*, 208
—, Pyramidal, 211
—, Spotted, 210
OROBANCHACEAE,
  184
Ox-tongue, Bristly, 147
Oxalis acetosella, 71

Pansy, Wild, 51
Papaver rhoeas, 30
PAPAVERACEAE, 30–
  33

Parsley, Beaked, 111
—, Fool's, 107
—, Hedge, 107
Pea, Grass, 88
—, Yellow, 87
Pearlwort, Common, 52
Penny Cress, Field, 42
— -pies, 105
Pennywort, Wall, 105
Perforated St. John's
  Wort, 67
Periwinkle, Lesser, 171
Petasites hybridus, 139
Pheasant's Eye, 20
Phyteuma tenerum, 155
Pickpocket, 43
Picris echioides, 147
Pig-nut, 112
Pimpernel, 170
—, Scarlet, 170
Pinguicula vulgaris, 172
Pink, Maiden, 49
PLANTAGINACEAE,
  200
Plantago media, 200
Plantain, Lamb's-tongue,
  200
PLUMBAGINACEAE,
  198, 199
Polygala vulgaris, 48
POLYGALACEAE, 48
POLYGONACEAE, 202,
  203
Poppy, Common Red, 30
—, Horned, 32
—, Welsh, 31
—, Western, 31
Potentilla anserina, 93
— *reptans*, 95

Potentilla sterilis, 92
Poterium sanguisorba, 97
Primrose, 166
Primula veris, 167
— *vulgaris*, 166
PRIMULACEAE, 166,
  167, 169, 170
Prunella, 193
— *vulgaris*, 193
Pulicaria dysenterica, 132

Queen of the Meadows,
  90

Ragged Robin, 58
Ragwort, 142
Rampion Round-headed,
  155
RANUNCULACEAE,
  17–27
Ranunculus aquatilis, 21
— *bulbosus*, 22
— *ficaria*, 23
Rattle, Yellow, 187
Reseda lutea, 45
RESEDACEAE, 45
Rest-Harrow, 78
Rhinanthus minor, 187
Rocket, Sea, 46
Rorippa nasturtium-aquati-
  cum, 34
Rosa canina, 98
ROSACEAE, 89–100
Rose, Dog, 98
—, Rock, 47
Rosemary, Wild, 165
RUBIACEAE, 120, 121,
  124, 125
Rubus fruticosus, 91

Rumex acetosa, 203
— *sanguineus*, 202

Sand-Spurrey, Red, 63
Sagina procumbens, 52
Sainfoin, 81
Sandwort, Sea, 53
Sarothamnus scoparius, 72
Saw-wort, 144
Scabious, Field, 126
—, Sheep's-bit, 157
Scrophularia nodosa, 185
SCROPHULARIACEAE,
    183, 185–188, 190
Scurvy-grass, Common, 40
Seablite, Annual, 201
Self-heal, 193
Senecio jacobaea, 142
— *vulgaris*, 140
Serratula tinctoria, 144
Shepherd's Purse, 43
Sickle-wort, 193
Silene dioica, 55
— *vulgaris*, 54
Silverweed, 93
Sinapis arvensis, 39
Snowdrop, 216
SOLANACEAE,   179,
    181, 182
Solanum dulcamara, 179
Solidago virgaurea, 127
Sonchus arvensis, 152
Sorrel, Common, 203
—, Wood, 71
Sowthistle, Corn, 152
Spear Thistle, 143
Speedwell,   Germander,
    190
Spergula arvensis, 60

Spergularia media, 57
— *rubra*, 63
Spurrey, Corn, 60
—, Saltmarsh Sand-, 57
Stellaria holostea, 56
Stinking Hellebore, 25
Stinking Willie, 142
Stichwort, Greater, 56
Stork's-bill, Hemlock, 69
Strawberry, Barren, 92
—, Wild, 94
Suaeda maritima, 201

TAMARICACEAE, 66
Tamarisk, 66
Tamarix gallica, 66
Tansy, 136
Taraxacum officinale, 151
Teasel, Wild, 123
Thalictrum flavum, 17
Thistle, Musk, 145
—, Spear-plume, 143
Thlaspi arvense, 42
Thrift, 199
Toadflax, Yellow, 183
Toothwort, 184
Torilis japonica, 113
Tragopogon pratensis, 148
Traveller's Joy, 18
Trefoil, Bird's-foot, 76
—, Hare's-foot, 77
—, Hop, 83
Trifolium arvense, 77
— *campestre*, 83
— *pratense*, 82
*Tripleurospermum mariti-
    mum*, 133
Trollius europaeus, 24
Tussilago farfara, 138

Typha latifolia, 206
TYPHACEAE, 206

Ulex europaeus, 74
UMBELLIFERAE, 106–115
Umbilicus rupestris, 105

Vaccinium myrtillus, 164
VALARIANACEAE, 122
Valerian, Spur, 122
Venus's Looking-glass, 161
Veronica chamaedrys, 190
Vetch, Bush, 85
—, Horseshoe, 80
—, Kidney, 86
—, Tufted, 84
Vetchling, Meadow, 87
Vicia cracca, 84

Vicia sepium, 85
Vinca minor, 171
Viola odorata, 50
— *tricolor*, 51
VIOLACEAE, 50, 51
Violet, Corn, 161
—, Sweet, 50
Viscum album, 116

Wahlenbergia hederacea, 160
Wake-robin, 207
Water-lily, Yellow, 29
Whortleberry, 164
Willow-herb, Rose-bay, 102
Woad, 41
Woodruff, 125
Wrest-Harrow, 78

Yarrow, 135

PRINTED FOR THE PUBLISHERS BY WILLIAM CLOWES AND SONS, LTD.
LONDON AND BECCLES
920.469